Rational Animals

The Adventures of Ferd Rhino, Doc Bonn Koala, and Pauley Polar Bear

Professor James Perry

ISBN 979-8-89112-455-4 (Paperback)
ISBN 979-8-89112-456-1 (Digital)

First Edition

Covenant Books
11661 Hwy 707
Murrells Inlet, SC 29576
www.covenantbooks.com

Dedicated to my grandmother, Rebecca Allen
and my parents, Joetta and James Perry

Edited by Susann M. Sawyer
Master of Fine Arts

Contents

Prologue 1

Humans as Stewards of Nature 5
The Last Male Northern White Rhino Lives with Me, and a Koala and a Polar Bear too 17
Being Rational is a Choice for Humans 28
The Night the Animals Arrived 37
How it Happened 45
Seeing is Believing 55
Overcoming Fear 62
Being in the Wild 66
Bright-Eyed Sages 70
Let Your Conscious be Your Guide 74
Protecting Our "Self" Against the Illusions Created by Humans 84
What is Rational 100
Understanding Ontologies of the Things-in-Themselves 105
The Media Should be Objective, Not Subjective 113

Life in the Wild 121
When You Die, Your Soul Flies 125
Beyond the Shadows and Illusions 134
Noticing Your Authentic "Self" 137
Protecting All the Animals 143
Rational Beings Are Aware of "Self" 150
God Needs Humans to Protect the Animals 157

Epilogue 159
Suggestions for Further Readings 163

Prologue...

I have always done my best to support my fellow animals. I strive to be a logical human, and like most humans, I am very passionate about animals. I cannot imagine a world without animals. Nor would I want to. Most humans feel the same way. Animals have a soul and spirit just like you and me. Yet, supposedly, "rational" humans continue to destroy the animals and the planet every day.

One night, I dreamed I met a rhino.

"Walk with me," the rhino said. "Imagine yourself existing as a rhino like me as we walk and talk on the Serengeti Plain of Africa. Get to know me, and you will see I am a lot like you, and you are like me," said the rhino. "It is through our similarities that we will see that we love life and food; contented is what we seek to be."

"Amazing!" I thought. "A talking rhino. I shouldn't have eaten that pizza so late last night."

"Two roads diverged in a yellow wood," said the rhino. "I took the one less traveled by, and that has made all the difference."

"That's Robert Frost!" I said.

"Yes!" the rhino answered.

I knew the rhino was right, and so was Robert Frost.

You need to choose your paths in life wisely. You never want to travel too fast or without focus as you may miss the highlights of life that really make it enjoyable. Let alone, the paths you ultimately take become your reality. Choose your paths and roads wisely, as there are many tributaries in life.

"Turnarounds and backtracking happen all the time out here on the plain," the rhino said. "I have a friend who is a magpie – a crow, who leaves a trail of breadcrumbs everywhere he goes. He is always easy to find if you want to see him. You just follow the breadcrumbs and you can meet him. He is very friendly and has a loud, cackling voice. I sometimes follow him to find new watering holes. There is no need to hurry. I usually mosey more than walk – grazing. I take my time living here under the hot Sun on the Serengeti Plain.

The rhino told me what to expect as we walked along the edge of the plain.

"There are many animals here that you will see," the rhino said, "but there are not nearly as many as there used to be. Humans came and destroyed our natural resources. Now, the animals struggle to survive in order to just Be."

We need to remember that humans are animals too. At times, they act like it, which proves it. Human animals are not always rational or logical. Sometimes, human animals are irrational and illogical. They choose hate and violence over charity and peace. Humans and animals suffer and die in the process.

Humans have poisoned Nature with technology and industry. There are too many chemicals, too much cancer, and too much building for the sake of building, and not nurturing. Urban and industrial sprawl are depleting the animals' and humans' living spaces and destroying our planet.

The rhino explained that he was an ambassador for the animals in this region. "I want to introduce you to two friends of mine later who are ambassadors for other regions of the Earth – a koala from Australia and a polar bear from the Arctic Circle."

"Do they talk and speak English as well?" I asked.

"Oh yes!" said the rhino.

I ask the rhino if he had read the philosopher Martin Heidegger's statements about humans being Stewards of Nature.

He immediately said, "Yes... I love his work on humans and animals 'Being' in Nature."

All I could think was a rhino who reads Heidegger – I must be dreaming! And then I woke up...

I remembered Heidegger tells us that we should look to the behavior of the animals in order to see ourselves in the animals, and them in us. We should imagine our life as them, and them as us. Which animal are you? Which animal(s) denote your "self" the most or least? Which animals are your totems? These are important questions if you want to understand the animals and your authentic "self" Being within Nature.

The traits animals and humans have that are similar join us together. Our differences make us who we are. We should notice, acknowledge and admire the animals' simplicity within nature, existing to live free with no other intention.

Humans as Stewards of Nature. . .

To know "self" is to see your "self" existing outside of your wants, needs, and desires – simply, within Nature. Humans should build within nature, not on top of nature. To see your "self" away from the whirlwind of society is what matters most. Animals are a significant part of our world. Humans love animals. They should be protected accordingly. Most people care and want to make a positive difference in life. It is a few immoral and evil humans that make life hard for us all. It is obvious that the majority of humans do not want animals unnecessarily harmed. The humans need to speak for the animals because the animals cannot speak for themselves.

In 330 BCE, the Greek philosopher Aristotle stated that in striving for goodness and "virtue" in life "rational" humans are seeking a self-fulfilled life of "happiness" here on Earth. It is the goal of the virtuous humans to engage in "thinking-about-thinking" and "critical thinking" in order to insure they have a virtuous life of happiness. All animals seek contentment – just as human animals do. You cannot be content without happiness. The human animal is on Earth to be the "animals' animal."

The goal of the contented, rational being is to live with virtue, goodness and happiness through brotherhood and sisterhood with charity and love. Without the rational search for virtue with goodness, humans will destroy themselves, right along with all the other animals. All animals share a universal soul with each other, and it should not be senselessly destroyed. When we extinct or harm animals, we are actually harming ourselves. Every being has an individual spirit and soul, and we are all connected; therefore, it is our duty to protect the animals.

On Earth, the primary duty of humans is to be Stewards of Nature. This means protecting all our Natural Resources including humans, animals, plants, water and rocks, right down to the sand – all the things that we utilize in order to live decently in life. We must protect and nurture the animals. These resources allow us to provide food and shelter that is necessary for our survival. Humans are here to protect all resources in order to insure nature is not interrupted or destroyed by reckless and irrational human activities.

Our natural resources exist within nature "at-hand" for our usage. These resources should not be exploited. The resources we have should be utilized pragmatically and ergonomically with vision and not with blindness and profit margins. The resources, the humans, and the animals must be protected.

Technology that was meant to help us has harmed and separated us. Industries that we have created are destructive towards life. The Sun, Moon, Wind and Water provide us with energy sources. We must harness these energies better in the future. We must respect and understand these resources as they are key to our survival on this planet. If the animals and their habitats keep disappearing, Earth will die and so will all its inhabitants.

Spring water comes from the ground. The spring water is here for us to drink if the water has not been contaminated. But rivers and streams have been contaminated by humans. This includes the lakes and oceans. There are warnings for eating fish from all these waterways. It does not matter if it is a pristine, glacial lake in Michigan, Wisconsin, New York, or a river in Ohio, New Orleans, Phoenix, or LA; they are all poisoned. Adults can eat one meal of fish per week. But no fish for pregnant women, infirm people, and small children, especially under the age of two. Humans are not supposed to eat bottom feeding fish at all. But they still do. The fish are contaminated with mercury, arsenic, lead, nitrates, solvents and other chemicals from farming and industrial runoff.

We are 'extincting' ourselves right now – this minute – as some corrupt humans insure the death of nature for their own profit. They know what they are doing as the purveyors of death for money. The time has come to recognize these individuals and the groups of which they are a part that do evil to us all. Many of them are connected to politics. These evil ones do not care who they kill, as long as it is not them or their own. The evil ones are worse than the lowest irrational animals. The goal of the evil ones is to live and die with the most money. It sounds irrational, does it not? There are no pockets in a coffin. These evil ones are driven by materialism and greed and not the preservation of life.

The evil ones "say" they care, but it is lip service to the people to make the evil ones look sincere. Since the evil ones do not care about human or animal life, let alone the life of the planet, it is up to those rational humans who read this book and see the wicked ways of the evil humans to make positive change. Humans need to stop the animals and the humans from dying in vain.

When people only care about money and materialism there is something wrong. With all the irrationality and evil around us, we must continue to remember that humans have rationality to allow us to think critically in order to preserve nature and create positively. Instead of destroying the animals and ourselves, we must act now to protect the animals who cannot speak for themselves.

Humans possess the ability to be rational, which means we can stop irrationality and evil, but, as we know, humans do not always use rationality. Some evil humans use rationality to harm others intentionally. We know some humans are striving for virtue in life and trying to lead happy lives through rationality while helping others along the way.

The irrational and evil ones are not striving for goodness and virtue in their daily lives. They are striving for money and control over the masses as a means to an end. They will never obtain it. They are in politics and media. They want your money. They want your life. They have no soul. We must not use virtue as a vehicle to make money or obtain happiness. Money is the filthiest thing on the planet, literally and figuratively. So are the humans who live for it. We must strive for virtue in and of itself and seek goodness in order to live in happiness. If we are not striving to be good, we are living wrong.

Irrational humans seek wealth and power over goodness and virtue. Because of it, they never fully obtain virtue or goodness, let alone, happiness. They remain unfulfilled while they seek more and more money. They seek to control their world and yours. They seek to control the "entire" world. Their lives become an egomaniacal, vicious cycle. They do not care who they harm. People and animals are dying worldwide while the maniacal ones profit off their deaths. The "money" becomes an addiction for the irrational and evil people, as they have brainwashed their "self" and anyone who will listen to them. They have deluded their "self" into believing they are actually "good" people when they are not. In other words, they believe their own lies.

It is outright absurd that a few irrational and evil humans with great wealth should be allowed to kill humans and animals daily with human-created viruses and biochemicals that destroy entire species of animals for profit in the name of politics. But it is happening.

Aristotle tells us that the essence of being a human is using rationality to its fullest degree through thinking-about-thinking. We exist as humans to be rational through critical thinking. We should engage in thinking-about-thinking in order to protect ourselves and the other animals.

Ultimately, utilizing rationality is the highest good a human can do on planet Earth, and it is the only thing that can save us and the animals. Our authentic purpose as human animals is to use rationality to protect ourselves and each other while seeking virtuous lives of happiness on Earth.

As I said, humans are the Animals' Animal. Yet, some nefarious humans do not care. Evil humans profit off the pain and suffering of other humans and animals. These evil humans misuse rationality to harm unsuspecting others. These evil ones appear rational to make others believe in them. They lie and make false promises never revealing that they choose personal wealth over other individuals and humanity. The evil ones are no better than sophists and charlatans.

And you do not want to be one of them.

The evil ones profit from the death of humans and animals. This is completely wrong, and it has been going on for far too long. All life should be protected and not harmed for nonsensical reasons. The proper usage of rationality in a positive and virtuous sense is what puts human animals above the rest. Without rationality there will only be more unnecessary death.

We must become familiar with the habits of the evil humans who harm nature for money so that we can terminate their destructive activities. These evil ones exist in all sectors. They could be wealthy or poor, appear good or bad, and not be. At the end of the day, their goal is to appear caring, or as good business people, while they destroy anything and everything to make money. They wish to bolster their bank accounts and their personal lives, which is most usually guided by money and their own "conjecture." They will deny it. But the truth will be found in the results of their actions within the outcomes of their manipulations of others' lives. Upon close examination, the illogical flaws of these evil ones appear.

Humans must change the way they perceive nature in order to protect it. All the rational animals are well aware of this; they just do not take part in the reflection of "self" to authentically see it. We are taught from a very young age that the primary goal of humans is to be benevolent and good to others and our "self" as well as all things in Nature. This includes all the natural resources we use in our survival. Humans should only take what they need for survival and not senselessly destroy Nature. Now, more than ever, it is extremely important that rational and logical humans recognize the harm we do to each other, the animals and nature itself on a daily basis.

When it comes to endangering and extincting animals, humans care, but the animals still disappear. In the end, animals are senselessly and needlessly killed by humans, be it by accident, or on-purpose, as with poaching, when animals are killed for ridiculous myths and legends. Nonetheless, the end result is the same; animals continue to go extinct as they experience more and more pain.

Look around your "self" and notice what you see – hatred, violence and pain. Notice the politicians feeding lies to you through their media allies. The day will come that the irrational actions of others will affect your ability to Be. Today is that day. Eventually the good humans will stand up against the tyranny. But how many will die in the meantime without the proper usage of rationality?

Many humans are already dead and dying, and many animals are threatened and already extinct. These animals will never be seen again, except for pictures in a book, or online, which is no way to see a Northern White Rhino, a Koala, or a Polar Bear if you really want to get to know them.

All living things have individual "Being" on Earth. Every living thing also has a presence as a "being" on Earth. All things existing together are "beings" on Earth. Every "being" on Earth is meant to be here. Our unique spirit and soul with which we are born makes it so. Every being (animal and human) has (an individual) "Being" that makes up their lives as "beings" existing together on Earth and within the Universe. Every being is sacred. None are better than others in the eyes of the God. We are all equal. To find our individual, authentic, human "self" and be at peace with others is what rational humans seek.

Every year, hundreds of rhinos are killed for their horns in South Africa by poachers, and the horn is nothing more than keratin. Keratin also makes up human fingernails and toenails. Every year, over 1,000 rhinos are killed worldwide for keratin. There is no chemistry to keratin; it is an inane substance. The rhino horns are ground up and sold in Asian and Middle Eastern countries on the black market due to an ancient belief (legend) that the horn is medicinal, that it is an aphrodisiac, that it builds virility, and strengthens male potency. None of this true. The rhino horn as medicine is a complete myth, an illusion created by humans to make money while rhinos are slaughtered unnecessarily.

All animals are connected to each other and to all humans. When we allow animals to be senselessly harmed and killed, let alone, become extinct, we are only harming ourselves. The good and rational people must act now to bring aid to all endangered animals before it is too late; we are the only ones that can change the animals' fate.

The Last Male Northern White Rhino Lives with Me, and a Koala and a Polar Bear too...

I remember seeing the Northern White Rhino at zoos when I was a child in the late 1960s. They were the largest of all rhino weighing in between 5,000 and 6,000 pounds or 2,721.5 kilos. In my lifetime, I have seen the Northern White Rhino become extinct. In 1969, there were 20,000 Northern White Rhino; now there are only two elder females left, Najin and Fatu.

The last male, Sudan, father of Najin and Fatu, died in 2018. When Najin and Fatu die, all the Northern White Rhino will be gone. This means the Northern White Rhino, weighing 5,000+ pounds, standing over 6 feet tall, which has existed for over 15 million years, has completely been erased from Earth within a 50 year time span. This is how humans destroy animals and themselves. It also mimics what humans do to each other every day. Not only is this wrong; it is senseless, immoral, illegal and unethical.

Sudan is pictured about six months before his death from old age. He was believed to be the last male Northern White Rhino.

The Sudan photo, taken at Ol Pejeta Conservancy in Kenya, is courtesy of Ami Vitale.

In my lifetime, one of the most majestic, prehistoric animals on Earth has disappeared.

The last male Northern White Rhino is gone. Or so the world thinks…

The truth is that the last male Northern White Rhino lives with me. His name is Ferd – Ferd Rhino. Sometimes I call him Ferdo Rhino. And sometimes I call him "Ferdy" just to tease him. He always yells out at me, "Jame!" – short for James, and he always tells me to "Stop it!" But then he laughs. I think he likes it!

Ferd's best friends are Doc Bonn Koala and Pauley Polar Bear. All three of the animals live with me, and it is one happy menagerie! The animals' "soul" mission in life is to help others. They exist to stop abuses of power and injustices that harm the animals – human and otherwise. Humans are not only responsible for our survival as humans; we are responsible as caretakers of all living things on Earth.

All that being stated, I present Ferd the Rhino. Ferd is one majestic rhino. Ferd is very large and he has a giant head, with a horn that is scary big. Pointy too!

"Thank You!" Ferd said. "I always like to have a good point, especially when I speak. It allows me to be more persuasive!"

As you can see, Ferd has a vivid sense of humor. His horn is his pride. I cannot imagine people killing rhinos to steal their horns. Some humans have a lack of authenticity towards life and their actions show it. Poaching is illegal. More than that, it is ethically wrong.

"I can see my horn just as clearly as the nose on 'face'; actually, my horn obscures my nose a bit," Ferd said, laughing and clanking his teeth together making a wooden sound.

I told him that it sounded like his head was hollow.

"It is hollow!" Ferd chuckled. "I use it to ward off troublemaking humans and animals!"

The chomp-chomp of Ferd's big, round teeth does the trick. I told him it was bone rattling to say the least. It startled me.

"See!" Ferd said. "I told you – self-defense! It is the way. Think critically and protect yourself and help others along the way. That is what life is about every day!"

Ferd is right you know. There is so much poaching on the Serengeti Plain of Africa that it is hard to imagine being Ferd Rhino or any other animal trying to survive out there with all that impending doom and death.

"When you are in-country, and you grew up there, you know death is part of life and it happens every day," Ferd said. "Death on the Serengeti Plain is part of life. We were born in the struggle of the food chain. We accept that. But now with human animals encroaching on our lands with urban and industrial sprawl and senselessly killing us, we don't have a chance without human intervention."

Amazingly, Ferd, Doc Bonn and Pauley have the ability to change their sizes. When they are small, which is most of the time, Ferd and Pauley are about five inches tall, and Doc Bonn is about three inches tall. They are voracious readers and they love learning. They also love food and eating! I always encourage Ferd, Doc Bonn and Pauley to eat when they are small because if they ate when they are full size, I would be broke in a week – $$$! The animals are perfect in form and function and true to their authentic nature.

Ferd, Doc Bonn and Pauley have to get "big" for about five to ten minutes each day when they become their regular, wild animal size. It allows them to stretch out and meditate. When we are at home, which is most of the time, they get big a few times every day. The animals can also make themselves invisible, and they can levitate too!

I remember a day, years ago, when I walked into the living room, and Ferd stood in the middle of the room with Pauley beside him, while Doc Bonn chewed eucalyptus, conversing amongst themselves. The three were full-sized and the floor was creaking – what a site! With Ferd Rhino at 5,800 pounds, or 2,494 kilos, and Pauley Polar Bear at 1,300 pounds, or 590 kilos, and last, but not least, Doc Bonn Koala coming in at 21 pounds, or 9.5 kilos, I was afraid the floor might collapse.

“I try to be smart because I am small,” Doc Bonn said. “As I always say, think big when you are small, and stay in your own tree!”

Over time, it was apparent that Ferd, Doc Bonn and Pauley are definitely in the right place living with me. When they came to me, they were only a year old and headed to the zoo. Then they showed up at my door. I have grown so attached to them that we are like family. We are brothers from different mothers. I help them every way I can, but we still have technical problems with their abilities.

Ferd elaborates… “We can control the size changes, and get small in a nanosecond, but we have less control when we are getting big. Over time, things have smoothed out, but not always. Sometimes one of us just suddenly balloons up to full size. It is actually quite amazing, but we try not to brag. I usually just shout out, Stand Back! A little more room please..."

In the beginning, the animals could make themselves small at will, but when they had not been large for a time, they would feel the urge to get big, and there was nothing the animals could do to stop it. Boom! It happens! And the animals are full size, more like supersized. The animals needed to work on these tendencies as it could save their lives and also be a detriment. I explained they could be harmed or killed if they do not control their size changes.

Ferd, Doc Bonn and Pauley were suddenly very concerned.

"It will be alright," I said. "Things take time. We will figure it out. We must have faith in one another."

The animals agreed!

There was flurry of hand and paw shaking, and lots of hugs, including a few bear hugs! Doc Bonn was small but very intelligent, Pauley was big, very Big, and Ferd, well Ferd, he was H-U-G-E!!!

"Y'all are so majestic in your 'animal-ness!'" I told them, "You are absolutely wonderful animals, and now you have rationality and all these special powers – amazing!"

Then things got quiet, almost meditative, compared to the ruckus that had been going on as the animals shrunk back down to their small size. It was unbelievable.

Doc Bonn said, "I don't want any special privileges because I am the smallest; just treat me equally!"

Ferd said, "Bonn, you are an equal, you have a heart 10 feet tall, and you are an animal! Just like us!"

All the animals laughed! I picked up Ferd and Doc Bonn and set them on the table.

When I picked up Pauley Pola Bear, he yelled out and laughed, "It tickles! It tickles!"

It is obvious how wonderful these animals are. I knew I had to take care of them at all costs to insure they are protected. We need to help all the animals – human and otherwise.

But 'how' is the question. Reading this book is one way to start thinking critically to find your authentic "self" and help the animals. Word of mouth works well. Talk to your friends about the problems of humanity. We must share the hardships inflicted upon all animals in order to bring awareness and stop the killing.

When I first met the animals I knew I had to keep them out of sight, but Ferd, Doc Bonn and Pauley were a rambunctious lot. I needed patience. But I usually have none – unless I am fishing. The animals were like me. No patience. Always talking. The fact is that "wild" animals do not always listen very well. Why? They're Wild!!!

One day, I laid a deck of cards in front of Ferd, Doc Bonn and Pauley. It was a "Go Fish" deck. Pauley was ecstatic over the proposition of anything involving fish or seafood!

"I am absolutely crazy over seafood!" Pauley exclaimed. "It is my life's blood! And a card game about fishin'? Well, that is absolutely fabulous! Yeah–us!!!"

I showed them the rules, and played a few hands with them to get them started. The animals were enthralled; they were wild, but they took to the game right away. Their rational side was showing, and it was not long until I heard, "Got any 3s? GO FISH!!!"

"We love this game," Ferd said. "We want to play it every day!"

I was not surprised. As a child, I loved playing "Go Fish" and "Old Maid," so it was great to see the animals having so much fun just Being.

But what does that mean? They are content in life. Ferd, Doc Bonn and Pauley are contented. They do not look outside themselves for happiness; they know they find that inside themselves. They are satisfied to be who they are and enjoy their lives. Humans should take a lesson. Look inside for peace of mind.

Being Rational is a Choice for Humans...

Animals live based on instinct within Nature; they do not attempt to live on top of Nature through "supposed" rationality as so many humans do.

With my guidance, Ferd, Bonn, and Pauley have become more rational than most humans. But they do not see themselves as superior. The three animals have all the knowledge of the animal world, the human world, planet Earth, and all that of the universe, just as all rational and spiritual beings do, if they stop to contemplate their own "self" while Being-in-the-World. You can have all that knowledge too, if you seek to read, research and write for your enlightenment. Of course, it takes years of research, reading and writing, and "meditation" to accomplish this, but that does not bother Ferd, Doc Bonn and Pauley. They love learning new things. They know so many things that they knew nothing about or knew out of context. During the early years with them, trying to understand things, we had more misunderstandings than you could count.

Over the years, I have really gotten to know these three animals for who they are and their needs. More than that, I learned from them, first hand, about how the animals feel when they are loved, and when they are mistreated and harmed or killed. Just as with humans, when an animal dies, a sadness arises and all the animals know.

Despite having rational abilities, many humans do not contemplate their authentic, personal, and spiritual self-consciousness very often, let alone, reflect upon it with any depth. For the most part, people are posers when it comes to living an authentic life because they look to others to see how they should be instead of looking inside. Many are unaware of this issue. In short, they do not seek authenticity. They rarely participate in introspection; they spend all their spare time with the others.

Many humans lack time with personal "self" away from the others to reflect and meditate.

These individuals lead hectic lives with little time for "self" spirituality. These individuals are confused and they rarely experience happiness. Without conscious change, they are doomed to unhappiness which is worse than death. Even animals know that.

Before Ferd, Doc Bonn and Pauley received rationality, they lived solitary lives in the wilderness. Now that they have rationality and the ability to participate in thinking about thinking, Ferd, Doc Bonn and Pauley are true scholars. The three animals are very well-rounded. They have the best of both worlds – being wild, and doing so with an education. Perfect!

Ferd, Doc Bonn and Pauley are trained in the Classics, Humanities and Philosophy. They love math and science. They understand alchemy. They believe in faith, hope, love and charity, open-mindedness and doing "no harm" to others. They also believe in God. They have "rational faith" that God exists.

"When you see the order and beauty of Nature it is easy to see that God exists," Ferd explained. "We must use our faith to stay positive and seek harmony."

As individual thinkers that existed in the wilderness in three different parts of the world under the chaos of Nature, Ferd, Doc Bonn and Pauley have insight into their lives that the humans do not see. They have seen life and death first hand. They have functioned and existed on gut instinct – lived by their "wits" if you will; it is the animal way. It is greatly the human way too. We should see our similarities with the animals in order to respect their Being and see where it intersects with ours. Through our similarities, we become one with the animals.

I explained to the three animals that human beings have gut feelings too, just as Ferd expressed. Humans are taught from a very young age to follow gut feelings in their decision making. But modern media desires to destroy rationality with propaganda. Usually children are taught to use rationality in order to protect their "self" in life. Utilizing rationality with gut feelings and critical thinking protects us in life.

But it is hard to tell what today's children know, learn or retain as they are fixated with everything they see, especially technology. Someone might ask why their parents never intervened and spoke to them about the dangers of technology.

Time is an illusion. Nature exists outside of time. The concept of time was invented by humans to keep us on time, or make us late. But "time" is not real; there is no clock in Nature. Animals do not keep time. They exist outside of time. Humans exist outside of time as well, but they are too busy keeping time to notice. In a sense, humans have sold their soul for time and clocks. No one likes living on a clock. The proof is in noticing how much more enjoyable life is when you are not being timed. Time goes really fast when there is no clock because humans enjoy existing without time, just like the animals.

Ferd, Doc Bonn and Pauley know their authentic "self" as they live in a state of "self-reflection" towards their spirit and soul. They have read Soren Kierkegaard's thoughts on Faith in God. Kierkegaard clearly stated in 1830 AD that it takes a personal "Leap of Faith" to see the face of God. To truly see God, you must believe. St. Augustine said it in 400 AD and St. Thomas Aquinas said it in 1260 AD. People have been saying it for thousands of years, yet some people still are blind. Faith must be carried by us continuously and nurtured by our "self" towards our spirit through daily reflection and meditation, or we may lose track of ourselves.

St. Thomas Aquinas' "Natural Theology" expresses that it is through witnessing the miracles we see on Earth that we See the Face of God. When we tell others of the miracles we have seen, we become ambassadors of God. The awareness that comes from sharing the miracles we witness affects our soul in a positive light. Our self-consciousness and self-conscientiousness towards Nature and God are renewed. This is what the philosopher understands. We have to deal with the chaos of Nature and bring order to it, but not abuse it in the process. By examining our "self-consciousness", we begin a reflective pathway to understanding our existence on Earth as beings with respect to our individual Being.

Ferd, Doc Bonn and Pauley have daily meditations towards "self" with deep reflection of their spirits. I meditate with the animals, and we discuss it later over green tea and crescent cookies. I have taught Ferd, Doc Bonn and Pauley that this is the only way to live intelligently above the fray of society. With meditation, we avoid the mindless rabble of life in order to protect ourselves. We move forward, we do not take prisoners, we just follow our dreams, and live to our full potential.

The rational human knows that the spirituality of life is constant. It never ends – 24/7. It does not only meet on Sundays and Wednesdays for an hour. Spirit is constant and in constant need of "self" maintenance. Many of those who do not reflect on "self" live day-to-day, often with little deep thought, running from one thing to the next.

They are a detriment to their own health and existence. When many rational humans lose their personal "self" while engaged in daily life, they have no chance at a happy Life. If your life is unhappy, perhaps you should think about why. Life can steal your personal focus. When rationality fades, so does the Light of Being. Darkness follows. The willful denial of reflection upon individual authentic "self" can be a fatal mistake if left unchecked.

"On the Serengeti Plain, my only thoughts were for myself and my friends and family; staying alive was my main concern," Ferd said. "Although I was fearless then, now that I have rationality I can see where I was foolish. The world is a very big place full of many beings all trying to survive. Every being matters, not just yourself. Humans and animals die every day just trying to stay alive. One must take care and beware in order to live another day."

To stay alive in happiness, you must contemplate your own existence. The positive reflection of "self" occurs as if you were looking in a mirror, once, twice, three times removed from your "self" and asking your "self": What do you see? How are you? What do you want? What do you need? Where are you going? When? Why do you do this, or that, in this or in that way?

Not only does this questioning of "self" build personal character, it lays a positive and personal pathway for the future. In this process, goodness will come to fruition for you, but only if you are virtuous in your endeavors. If you do not know who you are, how do you expect others to know you? How can you help others when you don't know yourself? Personal meditation is a key to spirituality that allows your inner "self" to see, reflect upon it, and authentically Be.

The goal of the rational life on Earth is to "Do No Harm" to others and take only what you need. Ferd, Doc Bonn and Pauley agree. Rational beings should strive for goodness and benevolence towards all living things, especially the animals who cannot speak for themselves. We must protect them. It is in striving for virtue that we get better and better as we walk through life. It is in the process of striving for goodness that we become more benevolent with the other humans and animals. When we critically examine our lives we get better and better in the process, but, unfortunately for all the goodness in the world, there is always evil.

The Night the Animals Arrived...

It was very late at night when there was a sharp and distinct knock at my door. When I opened it, Ferd Rhino, Doc Bonn Koala and Pauley Polar Bear were standing there. They were only inches tall. Ferd spoke to me directly in a loud, crackling voice. It was obvious that this little guy was all heart. He spoke to me like he owned the place.

"Hello... Hello there! My name is Ferd, Ferd Rhino!" He said, "I am a Northern White Rhino, we are escaping from the zoo, and my friends and I need a place to stay. We are cold and tired and very hungry. Could you help us?"

I could not believe my eyes or ears; the whole thing was surreal. "You are a rhino," I said. "You are a miniature rhino, and you are speaking to me in English. How did you get here?"

"It is a l-o-n-g s-t-o-r-y…" Ferd said in a diplomatic tone. "My friends and I are tired. Would you please help us?"

Doc Bonn Koala was standing next to Pauley Polar Bear who was nervously standing on one paw and then another, pacing like a polar bear would.

Doc Bonn said, "I hope this human will help us!"

Pauley said, "Yeah–us… I do not want to stay where we are not wanted. That is the worst thing to have to live where you are not wanted. That is as bad as being forced out of the Arctic Circle by humans. That was my home!"

Doc Bonn said, "I feel the same way about the Australian Outback! Animals are being threatened and made extinct by human animals more and more every day through urban and industrial sprawl. Most koalas end up as 'unnecessary roadkill' because of ignorant humans."

Then I heard Doc Bonn say to Pauley, "I sure hope this human is a good person. We really need help!"

Doc Bonn and Pauley were hopeful, but they were fearful too. After all, they were wild animals on the run. When I told Ferd, Doc Bonn and Pauley that they could stay, they ran right at me in a rush and hugged me. If they had been full size, I would have been crushed. They do not know their own strength. Even as miniatures, these are three strong, little dudes. And as full-sized wild animals, well, they need space. If you know what I mean. I will never forget that first night.

I heard Ferd say, "We are very lucky to have met a person who has an open mind. He seems like a very good human. He did not have to let us inside his home."

Pauley shouted, "I am just glad we found someone who wants us here. I do not want to live where I am not wanted. I am so hungry!!!"

As it turns out, Pauley Polar Bear is always hungry.

Doc Bonn said, "I believe in karma; we met the professor for a reason! He is not only going to help us; he is going to help all the animals."

When I met the animals, they did not have experience using rationality in the real world. Up to now, they resided on instinct and intuition as they existed in the wild. I know it is hard to believe, but it's true! These animals coming to me is the most precious gift I have ever been granted. Just knowing Ferd, Doc

Bonn and Pauley has allowed me to better see my authentic "self" as I exist in the world.

Even after being a professor for over 36 years, these three animals have helped to enlighten me. I truly believe Ferd, Doc Bonn and Pauley came to me by the Hand of God. They believe it too! They have faith. Faith is essential to living life. When you have faith in your "self" and faith in God, and know your mission, and you truly believe in something, nothing else matters.

No one can take your faith from you when you truly believe. The animals know that even when you are locked up in an enclosure at the zoo you are still free in your mind. Well, at least somewhat free in your mind because when you are locked up, it is hard to be free in any form of the word. But these animals were born free, and they were meant to remain free.

Ferd, Doc Bonn and Pauley were born to only live within their world and only face the natural predators they encountered. Humans are the worst predators. These animals were made to live in goodness without interference from humans. They were content with their lives. But humans showed up and changed that, and now we deal with the aftermath.

From the beginning, I told the three animals that they would be safe with me, but that they had to listen to me, or things may not work out so well. The three agreed they would listen. Little did I know of the spiritual "will to power" of these three fellas. Friedrich Nietzsche tells us, "The world is a will to power and nothing more. Go out into the world and live life to your fullest potential!" Ferd, Doc Bonn and Pauley were already supernatural beyond belief.

Before they got to me, Ferd Rhino, Doc Bonn Koala, and Pauley Polar Bear were in crates, on an airplane, flying to a zoo in the United States. They flew through an electromagnetic vortex over Boynton Canyon in Sedona, Arizona. The plane got caught in a severe storm with lightning, thunder, heavy wind and rain. The pilots lost control of the aircraft to a spinning altimeter.

"We might as well been flying through the Bermuda Triangle!" Ferd said.

"That's fantastic!" I said.

"I know, it's wonderful, isn't it?" Ferd replied.

I laughed out loud and said that I meant the entire story was incredible, unbelievable.

Ferd laughed, "Doof! Changing meanings blow my mind..."

"I get that, Ferd," I replied.

One thing for sure, Ferd, Doc Bonn and Pauley obviously have good senses of humor. They are not afraid to laugh at themselves – although they had a bad sense of direction escaping the airport towards the zoo. Or did they? After all, they made it to my house.

I explained to Ferd, Doc Bonn and Pauley that they should stay in the house and out of sight.

"You cannot go outside or you will be captured; you must stay inside because the zookeepers are looking for you," I firmly stated.

Obviously, Ferd, Doc Bonn and Pauley were relieved they had found someone who cared about them, and they thanked me again for helping them. But they did not seem to realize the levity of the zookeepers looking for them when the zoo was less than a mile away from my house.

I told them, "You are welcome here. I've always been a bit of an animal myself, so I relate!"

All the animals laughed.

The truth was that the zookeepers and police had driven down my street a number of times with search lights as they were actively seeking Ferd, Doc Bonn and Pauley. I did not want to concern the animals, and I knew they were hungry, so I changed the subject.

I know rhinos like to eat grasses and weeds or sometimes a cantaloupe for a treat. Koalas only eat eucalyptus, which is their sole food source. And polar bears love seafood, usually sea lions, 60 to 80 pounds each, they eat about six or eight sea lions a day when they are hungry.

I asked the animals, "Do you like toast?" What I got back was a giant question mark?

They did not understand, so I made some toast to show them. I explained, "Toast is bread warmed up, toasted, crispy bread, and people put things on the toast like butter, peanut butter, cheese, cream cheese or fruit preserves. Actually, people put anything they like on toast."

"Could I put fish on there?" Pauley asked.

"Of course you can," I told him. "Humans put seafood on toast points all the time!"

Pauley did a Polar Bear dance on his back feet. I was amazed. Wow! Could he ever cut a rug!

I told Doc Bonn there was no eucalyptus, but I would get some later. Doc Bonn said, "That is alright. I happen to have some in my pouch; I am never without it!"

You heard right; some male koalas have pouches. A koala is not a bear or a mammal. The koala is a marsupial; hence, the females have pouches for birthing baby koalas, and the males, well, some have pouches too. The koalas are utilitarian. Humans should take a lesson.

Doc Bonn Koala is very well educated, and he is extremely intelligent. Doc Bonn's practice is based upon the Hippocratic Oath, "Do No Harm!" Human doctors could take a lesson. Doc Bonn does not believe doctors should attempt to play God.

There is only one problem when you speak with Doc Bonn. You have to realize that koalas sleep most of the time. Koalas sleep up to 85% of the time. Doc Bonn says he is at about 80 percent most of the time.

He notes, "Domestic cats sleep more."

The koalas eat eucalyptus leaves which keeps them tranquil and sleeping most of the time. So you never know when Doc Bonn will drift off for a spell. Interestingly, even though he appears to be sleeping, he is actually still awake underneath, but only if you can pull him from his dreams. Doc Bonn loves sleeping and dreaming, and so do all the animals that truly Be in this Universe with You and Me.

How it Happened...

Ferd told the story of the transport airplane, the storm, and the electromagnetic vortex. To the animals, the vortex was even scarier than being in crates on their way to a zoo somewhere in the United States. Apparently, the turbulence and wind shear surrounding the vortex continued for over thirty minutes, shaking the airplane violently.

"It was the most frightening thing I ever experienced!" Ferd said. "I thought we would never get off that airplane alive."

Once the storm ended, and everything calmed down, the darkness disappeared, and a bright light shined upon them. The Light was Clarity. Rational Clarity. They were now "Rational Animals."

Ferd, Doc Bonn and Pauley would never be the same; they were now enlightened beings. Their first purpose in life was to seek virtue while utilizing critical thinking, just like humans are supposed to rationally do. The ability to rationalize facts over whimsical thinking is essential to our world. Ferd, Doc Bonn and Pauley have become masters of thinking. The ability to live by your wits through thinking-about-thinking and to approach life with charity and love over foolishness and hatred are the goals of all rational animals. These are the goals of Ferd, Bonn and Pauley – to live wisely and help others in need.

Although they did not know it at the time, the vortex had changed Ferd, Doc Bonn and Pauley forever.

Ferd explained they began to converse with language, first in their individual, native, animal language, which none of them understood, and then, amazingly, they were able to speak to each other, and they did so in English. On top of that, Ferd, Bonn, and Pauley were shocked to see they had been miniaturized to a very small size, so small they would now fit in a human hand. But this was temporary, as they became full-sized again shortly thereafter. Eventually, the animals would be able to control their size changes. To think of all this at once was too much, although they knew things had drastically changed.

Ferd, Doc Bonn and Pauley now had all the knowledge of the past and present plus common sense. And we all know that these days common sense is a Superpower. They understood that evil and irrational humans are the problem with our world.

Ferd, Doc Bonn and Pauley were now more intelligent than the majority of humans on Earth. They can see the future. Their powers come from their ability to reason through rationality, experience, and excellent observation skills. These three animals would never be members of a herd or follow like sheep. They are individuals first. Through rationality, Ferd, Doc Bonn and Pauley seek an understanding of individual and personal "self" with respect to God. They are a shining example of goodness and virtue on Earth. Ferd, Doc Bonn and Pauley Do No Harm to others. On the contrary, they seek to help others.

Their mission is to stop the unnecessary killing and poaching of animals. This includes human animals. Humans need to be educated. Human ignorance and unawareness are a blight on all our lives. Only humans can heal the planet and save the animals and themselves.

Animals like Ferd, Doc Bonn and Pauley are here to lead the way!

When Ferd, Doc Bonn and Pauley flew through the vortex over Sedona, Arizona's Boynton Canyon, they not only gained rationality, they gained a whole lot more. A vortex is an electromagnetic force on Earth that has been documented by pilots of aircraft, ships, and even people on the Earth itself. A vortex is described as a spiraling energy flow that changes time and space around those who experience it.

But Boynton Canyon is not the only vortex in Sedona, Arizona; there are others. These vortexes are best described as energy flows that give those who experience the vortex the ability to see beyond the worldly constraints of "self," beyond the Earth, into the Universe – to heal oneself through meditation and positive action towards individual, personal being through "self" realization and "self" actualization – to see the big picture of life as spirituality towards oneself.

For me, the energy within Boynton Canyon is strongest near a red-rock outcrop known to the Hopi Native Americans as "Kachina Woman."

Courtesy Photo/Public Domain

Kachina Woman references Hopi Native American ceremonies in which masked dancers appear. Kachina means "spirit father" in the

Hopi language. It is a reference to the Great Spirit or God. Humans have known about God for thousands of years.

"Your 'self' knows what it needs, but you have to feed it with positivity," Ferd explained. "My gut instinct tells me right from wrong and I follow my instincts. I use my rationality to protect and keep me strong."

"That is a very good philosophy, Ferd!" I exclaimed.

"Thank You," Ferd replied.

What a courteous and gracious rhino he is. I asked Ferd, "How do you know all these things?"

"Contemplative and meditative 'self'-conscience with personal conscientiousness towards God and Nature," he said. "Ohm... ohm... ohm..."

As Ferd began meditating with Doc Bonn and Pauley, they formed a circle, and they grabbed my hands on either side, and chimed in... "Ohm... ohm... ohm... ohm... ohm... ohm... ohm..."

It went on for 20 minutes. They were very good students. They say imitation is the sincerest form of flattery, but the words "over-characterization" came to mind. They were caricatures of me. "Unbelievable..." I thought, laughing to myself.

Ferd, Doc Bonn and Pauley are masters of their own destiny. Like so many humans, they are survivors. They have looked death in the face many times and have never turned back. Ferd, Doc Bonn and Pauley are winners. They keep moving forward; they do not take prisoners; they stay true to their abilities and gifts as beings on Earth. They are Renaissance Animals.

I asked Ferd, Doc Bonn and Pauley to explain what it felt like after they had flown through the vortex.

"We felt the same in many ways," said Doc Bonn. "But we knew things had drastically changed. We noticed right away that we had become unaffected by gravity, we were lighter, heavenly, and we felt Sublime. Personally, I never felt so good. We saw the Face of God."

Pauley exclaimed, "It was amazing, Yeah–us! We were floating in the air! Everything was out of control, and then the Lord showed up, and we were together in spirit. I never felt such peace or experienced anything so wondrous. Yeah–us!"

I remember the first time I gave Ferd, Bonn and Pauley cream cheese on toast with apricot preserves. It's one of my favorite foods from childhood. The three animals loved it, and things got very quiet as everyone was eating.

Then Pauley spoke up, "Wow! This is really good, Yeah–us."

Ferd asked Pauley, "Why do you always say 'Yeah–us?'"

"It is an affirmation of what we polar bears say to each other – Yeah–us," Pauley said. "It reassures and builds comradery between polar bears."

Ferd and Doc Bonn said that they completely understood comradery. Pauley thanked Ferd and Bonn for accepting his differences. But there was no need to thank them.

"We are as grateful for you, Pauley," said Doc Bonn.

Ferd, Doc Bonn and Pauley have learned to contemplate everything around them, all that happens, and everything they see. This is what philosophers do when they are seeking to Be.

In the beginning, it was overwhelming. Ferd, Doc Bonn and Pauley told me they were confused about what happened to them. Conversing with the three animals, we talked for hours, and they talked about everything!

I really had to listen because the words from the animals were very descriptive and real. I could not believe these three animals and their extraordinary memories. They remembered everything. There was an intellectual air to their discussion. Not a putting on of airs, but down to earth, intelligent beings discussing the nuances of "Being" on Earth. The animals' ability to reason through rationality was astounding.

But Pauley was running on instinct – food instinct. He made it very apparent that he was still hungry after two tins of sardines, and he was eyeing a third tin of sardines. Pauley looked at the image of a fish on the can of sardines with mustard sauce.

He asked, "Are these for everyone? Yeah-us?"

I told him, "The sardines are for everyone, and you can have them."

Pauley looked at the tin and read out loud, "Canned in Norway" – Pauley thought of the Arctic Circle, his home, now in danger because of human animals depleting the polar bears' hunting grounds through urban and industrial sprawl. Technology and industry we designed to help us are killing us.

Then Pauley said, "What is this can made out of, a-l-u-m-i-n-u-m-m-m?"

Then he gently split the tin lid with a polar bear claw, and mustard flew everywhere! What a mess! I explained, "The can is vacuum packed, so it is under pressure."

"We are all under pressure in this world!" Ferd said. "Human animals are trying to kill us! We must be vacuum packed too!"

All the animals laughed and laughed! And I just shook my head and wiped off the mustard.

Seeing is Believing…

Ferd explained that after their ordeal with the electromagnetic vortex at Boynton Canyon, they were exhausted. But once they knew they were to be placed in a zoo, they immediately devised a plan for escape. Still on the plane, Ferd, Bonn, and Pauley heard voices. They shrunk down as they hid themselves under the straw and foliage within their crates. They were so small they could fit in a human hand. Ferd, Bonn, and Pauley were frightened, but they had a plan. Their plan was that when the crates were open, they would slip out past the animal handlers. They were so small no one would see them.

"When we thought about living at a zoo, sadness came over us," said Ferd. "For us, it was darker than the darkest night. We felt like we were doomed. If you cannot live free, what is the point in living?"

The animals actually believed that if they had to be placed in a zoo, they would be better off dead. And nobody wants to think that!

"I used to live near the North Pole in the Arctic Circle, Greenland, USA, Yeah-us!" Pauley said with a grumbling polar bear tone. "I had wide open spaces and places to roam, and I come all this way to be confined to a zoo in an enclosure with a human-made pond. I cannot believe it! When I saw it, all I could think about was I want to go home."

Feeling the stress, Doc Bonn said, "Pauley, it will be okay!" Thank goodness for Doc Bonn's timing. It took everyone's minds off their dilemma.

When you truly get to know your friends, supporting them through tough times is everything.

When they met, Ferd and Doc Bonn had never seen a polar bear, but that was okay, because Pauley had never seen a koala or a rhino. Actually none of them had seen the other species before this event. It would have been geographically impossible before now.

The animals had differences, but they had similarities too. One thing they had in common was a love of life and good food! Yes, I said food. Like all living things, we need food to survive; it is our life's blood, right along with salt and water. All animals have to have food, salt and water to survive. Through noticing these similarities and respecting them, we become closer as humans and animals.

Ferd, Doc Bonn and Pauley accept each other for their strengths and weaknesses. They keep an open mind toward the others and new experiences, always striving to accept others. When things get them down, they stay positive. They never judge books by their covers. They read the books for themselves. They avoid stereotypes and prefer to meet and speak to others and decide for themselves how they personally feel about new acquaintances.

Ferd, Bonn, and Pauley avoid people who gossip. People who have nothing to say talk about other people. These three animals use rationality the way it was meant to be used – as a tool for thinking and reflection in order to live a good and happy life. They are using rationality to form relationships that promote virtue and goodness for all beings.

And they are doing it with a clear understanding of the frailty of life on Earth. Animals die every day and this includes human animals. But humans are in denial. The goal of life is to protect one another and not harm each other. We will only attain to virtue by striving for goodness. Ferd, Doc Bonn and Pauley know it's true and most humans do too.

Goodness brings Love and Charity, and Evil begats Hate and Pain, and Nobody wants to Die in Vain.

Ferd, Doc Bonn and Pauley understand that examining life is the way rational beings decide their futures. When I first started talking about this concept with the animals, they already had a keen sense of "thinking about thinking" as they were using it in daily life, but they did not step back and reflect upon it. They needed rationality for that.

"That's why we have rationality!" Pauley shouted. "I always love your lectures!"

I thanked Pauley for his kind words.

"Yeah-us" was all he said.

Do the animals and I live quietly? Are you kidding me? They call me "Dr. Dude-Little!" What do you think? Actually, it gets quite loud here at our home, but nothing is happier than the life we have together. The animals have come to understand that examining life through critical thinking is the only way to live a good life of happiness towards personal "self" as we walk through life.

Ferd, Doc Bonn and Pauley were born to be good. Humans are born to be good. But our circumstances and environment can change that. As we grow, our education and experiences change us, the world changes us, and some beings become evil in the process. Look at the human animals in business and politics today. It is a fact. The evil ones prey on the good people as they are generally unsuspecting of nefarious activities. Ferd, Doc Bonn and Pauley are here to make sure you realize who is here to help you and who is here to harm you.

Most humans strive for good their entire lives. By using rationality with critical thinking we may live virtuously with one another. We should never intentionally do harm to others, unless it is self-defense.

Ferd, Doc Bonn and Pauley use their well-honed gifts in order to live to their full potential in life. We are all gifted. We must find our gifts and polish them through practice and experience. Rational animals seek to be the best they can be in life.

"Goodness and Virtue! That is the way to Be!" Ferd exclaimed.

Doc Bonn and Pauley agreed, nodding their heads. We all know rational beings should be treated with respect. We should treat others with respect in hopes that they will treat us with respect and virtue when they act upon us. "Do unto others as you would have them do unto you" is The Golden Rule.

In 1780 AD, Immanuel Kant, the German idealist philosopher, believed that we are all born good. Evil is learned, either by circumstances at birth or from being raised in a bad environment. In "The Categorical Imperative," Kant stated, "Act according to the maxim of which you wish would be the universal if you were being acted upon."

As rational animals, Ferd, Bonn, and Pauley understand that being virtuous in the world means that rational beings should approach life with openness, goodness, and charity. They believe that rational animals should not act foolishly with hatred and violence. Unfortunately, a large portion of the world appears oblivious to these concepts.

Ferd, Doc Bonn and Pauley realize that Faith in "self" is akin to Faith in God. Faith is key in overcoming the difficulties and struggles in life. When they received rationality, the animals realized that they were alive for a reason, as we all are, and they truly believed that virtue and goodness in life are all that matter when you seek to live a happy life.

Doc Bonn explained to us that in his homeland of Australia, near Canberra, the wise koalas were known as "sage" koalas. One sage koala had instructed Doc Bonn and other young koalas on how to deal with feelings of fear. Of course, their teachings are all in koala-speak. But never fear, Doc Bonn is here to translate.

"I will continue to return until all sentient beings have become the best they can be," said Doc Bonn quoting The Bodhisattva from Buddhism.

The term bodhisattva refers to "a being who seeks awakening" – bodhi, "enlightenment" (or "full knowledge"), and sattva, "a being."

Doc Bonn explained, "The sage koala told us the goal in life is to help others while we strive to be the best we can be. We should exist rationally, while helping others along the way, each and every day. The sage koala also told us the best policy for life is to stay in your own tree and mind your own business."

All the animals laughed!

Overcoming Fear...

"Well, you know..." said Bonn. "Everyone gets scared, and everyone has fear, but you must not let your 'self' be overwhelmed by fear. You should channel thoughts of fear into positive energy in order to overcome negativity."

I told Doc Bonn, "The sage koala was correct to tell you this, but it is harder than it looks."

Having fear is a normal state of being. Anyone who walks through life thinking it is a safe place obviously does not engage in critical thinking enough to see the dangers. Having fear is a state of being; having the courage to get past fear is the goal. Strength in "self" and Faith in God make it so.

"You can say that again!" Doc Bonn replied, "I am always fearful of others, but I try not to be. Being a little guy with a rational mind helps me all the time. I see them coming to my tree, and I remain quiet until I see exactly how they are going to be. Personal reflection about life's situations is the way you see how you should live and Be."

Aristotle reminds us that human animals have fear, just as all animals have fear. But what really matters for humans and animals with rationality is how they adapt to fear in the real world. Aristotle stated that rational beings in fear often become "heroes", and those who think they are brave and those who are boisterous become "cowards" when fear is present.

Like most animals, Ferd, Doc Bonn and Pauley definitely understand the word fear. When they came to me, the world was a scary place for them. When they arrived, they were frightened of getting caught by the zookeepers. The zoo was no place for them. Even then they knew if they had faith in "self" and one another that they would succeed with their animal rights' mission to stop the needless poaching and extinction of animals worldwide. This is where we are now – fighting for all animals. But we fight for humans too – fighting for logic over emotion.

Although Ferd, Doc Bonn and Pauley did have a feeling of invincibility that night, danger was ever-present as they were mentally and physically in uncharted territory. Ferd, Doc

Bonn and Pauley were suddenly all very dependent upon one another for just about everything. Ferd, Doc Bonn and Pauley had each other, but they were all they had.

Suddenly Pauley said, “I do not feel quite right.”

They asked Pauley what was wrong, and before he could answer, Pauley began to shake and his eyes got very big and he said, “What is happening to me?”

Doc Bonn said, “Calm down Pauley. You are okay.”

And at that moment Pauley became full size.

“WOW!!!!” Doc Bonn shouted. “Try to remain calm...”

Right there, in a field by the airport, Pauley became his 1800-pound or 816.46 kilos self, and there was no hiding him. Thank God it was dark.

Pauley’s voice rumbled out from deep in his chest, “I am big again, please help me hide! Yeah-us...”

Doc Bonn told Pauley, “Lay down in the tall grass so no one can see you. It will be alright!”

As Ferd surveyed the landscape for humans, Bonn and Pauley looked around to see if anyone had seen them, their minds racing about what to do and then, miraculously, about three or four minutes later, Pauley miniaturized again. The three animals tried to figure out "how", but there was no apparent, easy solution. As they stayed there for a while, Ferd suddenly became full size too and then miniaturized after just a few minutes as well. Then it happened to Bonn.

"We do not know how often this will happen, or if we can control it," Doc Bonn said. "We had been small for hours before we became regular size again. Then we came back to small in minutes. We have to observe this phenomena as we continue on our path to Be."

As Ferd, Doc Bonn and Pauley sat in the tall grass that night, getting bigger and smaller, they began to get to know each other better as they spoke about their lives up to now; the animals realized they had things in common. One thing they had in common was that they were fortunate to have met each other, but, more than that, they were able to reflect and speak about their lives because of rationality. This was something they never could have done in the wild as their former animal selves. The animals could now speak and think about their individual Being as beings on Earth under Nature with respect to the Godhead. It was a truly amazing transformation.

Being in the Wild...

Ferd J. Rhino, the last male Northern White Rhino, was born on the Serengeti Plain of Africa. Doc Bonn E. Koala was born outside of Canberra, Australia. And Pauley Polar Bear was born within the Arctic Circle, Greenland, USA. Although all three animals were well experienced travelers, Pauley is the nomad of the group; he is a real wanderer. Pauley has swum and fished the northern oceans.

His motto is "Have Fish?" – "I'll Travel!!! Yeah-us!"

Ferd, Doc Bonn and Pauley have been taught to be virtuous while striving to live a good life of happiness. By existing as their authentic, individual "self" on Earth through critical thinking and reflection, they see their authentic "self" Being-in-the-World.

"When you walk through life, you have to be who you are!" Ferd explained. "You cannot walk through life pretending to be something you are not. It is too confusing, and, anyway, nobody likes a poser. To live a good life, we have to keep it Real!"

All three animals come from royal bloodlines, although they never act superior to other animals. They treat other beings with respect. Since they gained rationality, Ferd, Doc Bonn and Pauley question everything. They are aware that personal self-consciousness is accessed in different ways for different individual beings. Like all beings, the animals have the ability to contemplate their individual "self" meditatively in order to better see their Being as beings on Earth.

Rationally, we notice this part of personal "self" while we are in meditation and reflection of our spirit upon our self-consciousness and self-conscientiousness. Through this process, we see our deeper "self" awareness with respect to the other beings. We see Nature as it really is, not just as we perceive it. All animals, human and otherwise, exist spiritually within mind and body.

But, in reality, as the animals know instinctively, and humans learn through time, our spirits continuously seek to leave our bodies and soar to the heavens. This may lead to skydiving, bungee jumping, and other risky adventures, even death. Many are unaware that our souls survive death – that the afterlife is real. Our soul is immortal now. Our spiritual selves are eternal. Just like God. Our soul lives forever and so does our self-consciousness.

One distraction in life is guilt. Guilt is a part of life. Don't be guilty, seek virtue, and live free. Our mind controls our body in our endeavors; it keeps us on the path as beings. Stay positive. Avoid the negative.

Of course, our minds can also distract us. If we have logic and reason guiding us, the mind tempers the soul. If we are not logical and lack reason, we have no personal guidance system, and the soul has no reason to guide it. In this condition, many humans are not fit to live around as their lives are chaos just like their souls. If mind and body are not free, soul suffers and spirit withers and dies.

Many rational animals get lost between their own personal wants and needs versus the wants and needs of others within their lives. Being co-dependent in relationships and jobs is no way to live. In this position, co-dependent people may lose sight of reality. Here, personal "self" becomes obscured by the external world of the others. The individual "will to power" to overcome adversity becomes lost as the individuals are forced into a world not of their own. Instead, they are forced into a world created by others.

These others may or may not have known what they were doing when they created these worlds. But some individuals created these harmful worlds on purpose in order to profit from the unfortunate citizens they rob. Herein lies the problem. No one can live by whimsical doctrines dreamed up by ignorant and unaware people. This is not reality. It is made up.

The world today is frocked with illusions created by the others to make money off you. In reality, individual, rational beings should be creating their own world and living within it, first, and then grouping with the others to get things done. When you are in a group before you are an individual, your creativity is cut short by group-think, herd mentality. This is the first mistake against enlightenment to knowledge and wisdom. It is through individual, personal "self" that we become stronger than any group.

Bright-Eyed Sages...

Recently, when I woke from sleeping, the miniaturized Ferd, Doc Bonn and Pauley were lying right on my pillow. They always play cards late into the night, so when I go to bed they are still up playing "Go Fish!" You know... Pauley's favorite game. But they always end up in bed with me by morning – the gravitational pull of animals towards the warmth of other animals.

One morning when I woke I opened my eyes and Ferd was sitting up, staring right at me, looking very Spartan.

"Yes... What can I do for you, Ferd?"

"How are you?" Ferd said.

"I'm barely awake. How are you?"

Ferd responded, "I am great! Time to start a new day!"

And so it was...

Doc Bonn said, "Good Morning!"

And Pauley Polar Bear just said, "Mornin', Yeah-us..." And winked at me. What a character!

When Ferd speaks, he does so in a searing, crackling voice. "Hello!!! My name is Ferd! I am the last male Northern White Rhino! I am Lord of the Serengeti Plain, Stand Back! A little more room, please..."

I remember hearing Ferd speak the first night when the animals came to my house.

"My friends and I have escaped from the zoo, and we came here to see if we can live with you!" Ferd exclaimed.

I would have never thought such a commanding voice could come from something so small, but it did. And before I could speak, Ferd, like a carnival barker, introduced Doc

Bonn Koala and Pauley Polar Bear, who actually were quite gracious about the whole thing despite it being awkward.

I could not believe what was happening as Ferd, Doc Bonn and Pauley acted like they owned the place! I did not really mind as they were so interesting and amusing. They were downright loveable.

You see, Ferd is a very gregarious rhino, he is loud and somewhat boisterous, but, underneath, he is a full of love, although it was hard to see at first.

When he first entered the house, he shouted, "I cannot believe my eyes! We made it! The Eagle has Landed!"

I laughed out loud.

From the beginning, Ferd made it clear the animals' main concern is stopping the evil humans from poaching and killing all the animals.

"The world looks like a slaughterhouse from where I stand," Ferd said. "Too much death and destruction. It just isn't right!"

There is no doubt that human animals are poaching and killing animals daily at an alarming rate extincting the animals permanently, worldwide, and they are doing it for profit!

"If the humans do not quit extincting all animals, eventually, they will extinct themselves," Ferd said.

"We know that, Ferd, but the humans do not seem to care," I explained. "Apparently, many humans do not recognize all the harm they do to the animals and each other. Too many humans are building on top of nature instead of within nature. In the end, the humans will be the next animal to become extinct. And it will be at their own hands."

Without rationality and logical thinking, the human "animal" is just that, an animal. Humans must see past their differences and come together to help the animals and each other.

Let Your Conscious be Your Guide...

Poaching, killing and extincting animals are wrong. Humans do not eat exotic animals. This includes rhinos, koalas and polar bears. Shamelessly profiteering off illegal animal deaths has to be stopped. Killing animals and destroying nature with technology and industry are categorically ignorant.

A koala needs three trees in which to live, not just one.

"That's Right!" Doc Bonn said. "I need space to roam around and live the way God intended."

When humans encroach on koalas through urban and industrial sprawl, driven by the overuse of technology and industry, it is not just the fact that the koalas are vanishing. It is the fact that the koalas' habitat is being destroyed as well. When trees are cut within the koalas' habitat, humans suffer too. Unfortunately, many do not realize this fact. When the koalas lose their homes so do other animals of the forest. Less oxygen is produced in those areas. This is not just a bad situation for the koalas, it denotes less oxygen produced from trees, and our natural environment suffers because of human presence and interference. Humans are good at creating their own pain through bureaucracy.

I remember my grandmother started teaching me about conservation when I was old enough to walk. Her name was Rebecca. She loved animals and birds. She was an avid bird watcher and raised many animals on her farm. That farm was one happy place.

"We try not to kill living things here on Earth unless it is for food," she used to say. She raised and butchered her own chickens.

It would not be until I was seven that I would carry a single-shot .22 rifle as I was just beginning to go hunting for squirrels and rabbits with my father. I never felt bad about hunting, and I was taught to always give thanks to God for the food. I have never abused animals as they are more sacred than some people realize. How humans treat animals is a direct reflection of their character. I never met a human who had a roadkill incident, an accident, killing an animal that did not feel badly about it later. It is senseless to kill animals just because we can, let alone, for profit.

"That is why I'm fighting to stop unnecessary roadkill, worldwide!" Doc Bonn exclaimed. "We have to do something; animals are senselessly being killed every day. It has to be stopped!"

Doc Bonn is right that the abuse of animals needs to stop.

"We will never stop all unnecessary roadkill," Doc Bonn continued. "But by informing the public we might curtail it. We must act out of humanity, out of animality, for crying out loud!"

Doc Bonn gets very upset about unnecessary animal deaths, but that is good because somebody should. We invite you to do the same. Together we will make necessary change.

We all know that there is a "food chain" on Earth under Nature that has to function for our survival. Without the food chain and natural resources, we will all die. But the food chain does not include killing exotic animals like rhinos, koalas, and polar bears. It does not include poaching animals or killing for sport. Ferd, Bonn, and Pauley are here to help the humans see the error of their ways. The humans do irrational things that harm the animals of the world each and every day. How humans treat animals is a direct reflection of how humans treat each other. If humans continue to threaten and extinct the animals, in time, the humans will extinct themselves.

Just as I have taught Ferd, Doc Bonn and Pauley, individuals seeking virtue should exist in reflection of "self" as we walk through life as spiritual, individual beings on Earth, existing with all the other humans, animals, plants, and rocks, right down to the sand and soil – all our natural resources. Noticing and reflecting upon our experiences form the basis of our spiritual "self" as we see our authentic Being with respect to all the others.

Pauley immediately spoke up, "When I reflect on my authentic 'self' being-in-the-world, I see that I like to eat six or eight 60 pound sea lions a day when I am hungry!"

Bonn's eyes got very big as he said, "That is a lot of sea lions!"

Pauley replied, "It is. And I thank God for that! Yeah-us!"

All the animals laughed!

I reminded Ferd, Doc Bonn and Pauley that humans are born into this world with "apriori" knowledge. Apriori knowledge is what we have before we are taught empirically (aposteriori knowledge) by others in the external world. As we grow, the apriori provides a path to understanding our "self" as an individual Being. As we are taught and we learn empirically, our continued education aids in the maintenance of "self" and spirit while Being-in-the-World.

As we grow as children, the apriori and the aposteriori knowledge that we have and gain make us who we are as people. Our individual apriori essence at birth, combined with our aposteriori education – experiences and our environment – make us who we are as rational Human Beings.

Even the animals know this to be true. We should seek to adapt to who we are individually as we evolve outside of the other humans. This is accomplished by leading our "self" with thinking about thinking through personal reflection. In "self" reflection, we do not rely on the will of others. Here, we see ourselves. We have to participate with the others to get along in life, but we do not have to think like or emulate the others. It is far better that we think differently than the others, for if we all thought the same, nothing new would ever happen, and nothing new would ever be invented. We must keep an open mind.

"Correct!" Ferd said. "If we are not individuals first, life on Earth would be a very boring place."

It is always better to be one with "self" and our own actions before we attempt to commune with the others. We should always look within before we look outside ourselves. We should never hide who and what we are from ourselves. On the contrary, we should always be open to ourselves and to reflection of our spirit. We must be honest with our "self" if we are to live a virtuous life of Happiness. Lying to our "self" is the biggest flaw of humans.

The second biggest flaw of humans is lying to the others. Once rationality is misused to lie a path is cut. Look at politicians and media. The people who lie and create illusions of "self" will lie to the others for their own benefit. Here, the beginning is the same as the end – lies and more lies, straight into oblivion. Once the lies get started, they snowball, and become overwhelming for the liar. Eventually, the rational people see the lies and the ignorance of these individuals who believe they can lie and get away with it. But no one gets away with lying. They just keep lying until they get caught. Nonetheless, the lying individuals present us with a perfect image of how not to be virtuous and good.

The first rule of life that I taught Ferd, Doc Bonn and Pauley is that nothing human beings create is perfect. Even with rationality, no human creation is perfect. Humans are imperfect and they create imperfectly. We strive for perfection but never fully reach it. Plato knew this. Even when utilizing rationality to its highest degree, no human created thing is perfect. There is no perfection in life; we only make attempts at perfection by creating representations in the world from the ideas based in our minds. In the process, we get better and better as do our creations as we strive to be the best we can be, but we are never perfect. That is why when we get close everyone swears it's perfect – even though it's not!

Our creations may be close to perfection, but there are always flaws. When we create a chair, we believe it is the perfect chair. But the chair is not perfect. Someone else might build or prefer a different chair. Someone can always come along and say that this other chair is better or more ideal. So there is not an ideal because it is a subjective decision based on individual wants and desires. In subjectivity, we get lost. That is why the media wants you to be blind and listen to them.

So we create with perfection in mind, but never fully reach perfection when we create. This is why some things we build fail. We just get closer and closer to perfection with our creations and representations, but we never reach absolute perfection in the things we create. So when humans come along and tell you about how perfect their idea or plan is, remember this: Illusions and lies always have a grain of truth to rope people in; it's called "flash in the pan", if you will. It is designed to get your attention. Don't be a sucker. You'll thank us later.

"Now that sounds 'self' defeating!" Ferd said. "Striving for perfection when there is none. I do not like to be defeated by my 'self', Doof!"

"It's the thing your parents did not tell you, Ferd," I said.

"My parents were killed by poachers before they could teach me that," Ferd said with a tear in his eye.

"I know Ferd. I am sorry for that. Losing your parents to death is the hardest part of being a young animal. It is not much better as an adult," I continued. I reassured Ferd, Doc Bonn and Pauley continuously that we are all alright now and that is what matters most.

"Being content is everything," Ferd said. "Without contentment, we wander all our lives looking for something that does not exist. We have to look inside to See the best way for us to Be."

Bonn said, "That is exactly the way to be! Contented is the way for me!"

Pauley just said, "Yeah–us!"

There is nothing more devastating than the chaos of Nature. Yet, simultaneously, Nature has Order. This dualism of order and disorder within Nature is our biggest gift and our biggest threat on Earth. Humans are not God. Humans just like pretending they are God because of their egos. When humans attempt to become Gods, we are in serious trouble. In the end, living within Nature shows us the face of God. We cannot see the face of God by looking at other humans or their creations. We see the face of God through miracles.

By utilizing rationality, positively, through meditation, humans may see beyond their "self" in order that they may cognize and recognize their authentic "self" as beings on Earth. In other words, humans may see and notice who they are authentically on planet Earth. These reflective humans are positive, critical thinkers. But more than that, they are positive, spiritual beings at their core; they care. These rational ones seek "utility" in their lives. They respect the animals and nature; they don't consciously harm others. Rational humans seek "utilitarianism" when dealing with others. These rational individuals live with the philosophy of "Do No Harm" to others. They live and let live and harm as little as possible while they walk through this life.

Protecting Our "Self" Against the Ilusions Created by Humans...

As I explained to Ferd, Doc Bonn and Pauley, we try not to harm living things here on Earth. We only hunt and fish for food to allow us to survive. We do not kill for sport or for legends, or to feel superior. Ferd, Doc Bonn and Pauley have become well aware of this since they met me. Now, they are able to reflect upon their individual, personal Being and explore it with respect to the others and the world outside of themselves.

It is a Capital "T" – Truth of Life – that other than for food, humans should not kill living things on Earth. You only take what you need and you are thankful for it. You do not poach animals, kill for sport, or kill everything in sight just because you can.

Animals often are able to get along within their own species, and even get along with other animals outside of their species, but they operate on instinct alone, and there are always fights and scrapes in the animal kingdom, just like in the human world. Awareness tells the animals what they need to know and their minds and bodies make it so. Predatory and territorial relationships are part of the animals' survival instinct – protect "self", walk, hunt, gather, fish, swim, eat, and sleep. Of course, the vast majority of animals never have the opportunity to step outside of themselves and contemplate the lives they lead.

When I first explained this to Ferd, Doc Bonn and Pauley, they sat quietly looking into my eyes, hardly blinking as I spoke. They remained silent as I continued. When the animals listen to my lectures, they do so with a reverence for knowledge and wisdom. They respect wisdom and realize that no one owns wisdom; it is shared.

You can tell this as the ignorant and unaware people believe they own wisdom. They know the answers for you and them. They want you to follow along.

Ferd, Doc Bonn, and Pauley's good friend, a sparrow, is pictured. They call her the Sentinel. She is always on the lookout and reports in regularly. Everyone needs friends on the ground and in the air if they are to protect each other.

The sparrow, ever watchful, knows about humans who abuse "rationality" in order to make money off the others are the worst. These humans are evil in their endeavors as they regularly speak lies and harm others in the process. They make promises they cannot keep. They say that they are speaking the truth while they are lying. They have the ability to think critically and do good, yet they use rationality to harm animals for money and materialism. All the animals suffer—the rational human animals the most. We know better. It bothers us that we cannot right the wrongs of the world.

As humans cognize and reflect upon "self" with respect to the others, they realize life does not have to be this way, because with positive rationality, we see the lies and deceit from the evil ones. These evil humans destroy nature and make money off the process. These ignorant, evil ones are threatening and extincting animals in the name of money, power, and greed. They do not care for the others; they only care for themselves. Their lies prove it. In the end, they will destroy themselves just as they destroy everything they touch. We must act now before it is too late.

Ferd, Bonn, and Pauley suddenly all spoke at once. They asked: why would you use the goodness of rationality to do harm? The answer most of the time is to make money off those you harm with your irrationality. But a rational person seeks harmony. Life is a very long walk in the sun, and becoming enlightened can be frightening for some. The Capital T truths of life are not always positive or what we want to hear. Nonetheless, they are Truths. The pain and suffering on Earth are a very sad part of life. Fortunately, the Afterlife is real.

Being a professor of philosophy and having time to read, research and write have given me distance between the real world and the human created illusions within our world. These illusions come from all sectors. It includes everything from television commercials to religious and political agendas being cast at us constantly.

To discern the Capital T truths of life from the illusions created by humans is impossible without personal, critical thinking. But even with access to critical thinking, supposedly rational humans fail to exist positively as they still do harm to others for profit.

"Poaching rhinos for their horns kills my rhino friends, and it brings profit to evil humans," Ferd said. "The rational ones are abusive. Why? They have rationality but live irrationally. The humans create illusions that harm others. They harm animals and humans in the process. They seem to be unaware of goodness in the world due to selfishness. The good human helps care for the animals as the animals cannot speak for themselves."

"Unfortunately, that is correct Ferd. The illusions of life created by humans have been around since the beginning of time. Plato's 'Republic' written in 400 BCE tells us that a 'good life' is about striving for virtue and benevolence towards our 'self' and the others," I replied. "For Plato, 'the unexamined life is not worth living.'"

This means critical thinking has to be part of our daily existence. Life is about examining our lives as we walk through. In the "Allegory of the Cave", in Book VII of the "Republic", Plato warns us of the illusions some humans create in order to control others. Plato tells us that we should reflect upon our Being continuously as we walk through existence in order to get the most of our lives here on Earth. We should contemplate everything around us, including life and death.

Plato understood that our souls are immortal now and that people should seek the Light of Being on our own terms through critical thinking by examining "self" through

Nature. We should not seek answers to "self" by looking to the external world. The internal world of personal soul and spirit is where our answers lie.

The goal of the examined life is to live decently with happiness above ignorance and unawareness. From this position of contemplation and meditation, we may see the Light of Being while we notice our own position within existence.

Unvirtuous individuals, however, attempt to manipulate people into the false systems they create. Their goal is to control us as individuals and to turn our personal "self" into a group they can control. These evil, illusion-makers want to make you part of a "herd" as they cannot stand to have humans living with individuality. It makes the posers feel inadequate.

Media, government, business, politics, and religion are frocked with illusions from evil humans as they seek to harm people by removing the individual's "spirit" and "will" from the rational pursuit of critically examining life. And they do it all to make money off your Fears. These people seek power and control over others. They want to control you; if you do not follow along, they could kill you. Just look what they do to the animals that they extinct daily.

If humans are followers and not individual critical thinkers, when they come up against these evil ones, they will be doomed. The evil ones' goals are to make a group of human beings weak so that they can be ruled and controlled more easily.

Plato states that bad people will use the goodness of the benevolent people against themselves. The evil ones know you are focused on goodness, so they may predict your behaviors based upon that information. The evil ones know you will not be suspecting them as they lie to make you hear what you want to hear, not what they said. Many will lie and never deliver on their promises. These sub-humans do not even care about those that they harm and kill. They say they do, but truth shows in actions, not words and useless rhetoric.

We should examine our lives, and the matters of our lives, as we walk through life in reflection of our individual and personal spirit through "self" in order to live a "good life." We should not follow the illusions created by others as these illusions do not belong in our lives. These illusions have nothing to do with reality.

"Humans harm and kill us every day through their illusions and lies," Ferd said. "How can they call themselves rational animals and be this way?"

"Well... Ferd, Plato would say they are not rational. And they are not virtuous or benevolent. They are out to make money. The media knows nothing of virtue!" I exclaimed.

In "The Allegory," Plato tells us of a cave where human slaves have been held, chained together since birth. Plato states that the slaves are facing a wall, chained together, with their necks manacled so all they see is the wall they face. Behind the slaves, a fire burns. In front of the fire, and behind the slaves is a "parapet", where puppeteers walk on an elevated walkway carrying symbols or "representations" of real objects that we see in life.

As the puppeteers walk down the elevated walkway, shadows from the symbols are cast onto the wall in front of the slaves. The symbols mimic real life. Plato refers to this process, using the Greek word, as "mimesis", which means "mimicking reality." There is a danger here as humans may lose their "self" in viewing or participating in the mimicking of reality because they cannot tell fact from fiction. This is the position of the slaves.

The puppeteers' symbols include cutouts of humans, animals, fish, the moon, sun, and stars, flowers, trees, etc. When the puppeteers carrying these symbols walk down the path in front of the fire, the shadows of the false images they carry are cast upon the wall in front of the slaves. The slaves see the shadows and believe the shadows are reality-based.

But the shadows are only illusions cast by humans. The shadows are not real, yet the slaves do not notice. In this state, they believe in the shadows and the illusions, and the puppeteers become their masters.

"But your only master in life is you!" Ferd shouted. "Without our individual will, our lives are not ours!"

"You are right, Ferd! We must be individuals first if we are really going to Be in a world of confusion. And that's where we are – in a world of confusion."

The puppeteers are everywhere in our world. They control the masses with fear and illusions. Our world is full of them. They seek to control you as part of living out their dreams of power and control as money and materialism drive their illusions.

Outside of the reality of Nature, the world is greatly created by humans with all their pipe dreams, shadows and schemes, illusions, good and evil and everything in between. Some illusions are positive, some fairly real, but some are horribly evil that are used to steal and kill.

Plato states that a slave breaks free of the chains and emerges from the darkness of the cave into the Light of Nature. When leaving the cave, the slave is immediately blinded by the light. But soon, the slave's eyes adjust to the light, revealing many things in the real world. The slave sees the real Sun and Moon, feels the real Wind and Rain, and sees rivers and lakes, birds and insects, animals being, and fish in streams.

Pauley's eyes lit up as he said, "Did the slave eat some of the fish? I will help him catch some!"

Doc Bonn laughed, and said, "That figures! You are always thinking of fishing, Pauley!"

Pauley responded, "Yeah-us! I love catchin' fish and eatin' them!"

The levity of humor helps dire circumstances.

So when the slave gets outside of the cave and sees the real world, the slave begins to think about the world inside of the cave and how the two worlds differ. One world is created by humans. One is created by God. Humans only mimic God when they create. Humans are not God. Sometimes humans create positive things, but the negative things humans create demand more attention because the bad things hurt us the most.

Ferd, Doc Bonn and Pauley now understand the Truths about living a virtuous life. But they had to read, write and engage in critical thinking and research to become what they are now. Just because they were given rationality does not mean they do not have to strive and put forth the effort to utilize it.

Ferd, Bonn, and Pauley understand happiness, love and joy as well as pain and suffering and death. The animals know that the humans have no power over Nature even though they pretend to have it. Human puppeteers make their illusions so real that people cannot discern between reality and illusion, just like the puppeteers in Plato's cave who convey nothingness through the shadows and illusions they cast on the walls of the cave.

The "Allegory of the Cave" is not just about forcing people into slavery so they are controlled. It is about enlightenment upon the difference between reality and illusion – Truth. Plato reveals that some humans create shadows and illusions to make money off the other humans while enslaving them through brainwashing by illusion.

We have people like this in our world today within media, politics, government, business, and religion. They are in all sectors. Immorality is becoming common. Common sense is a Superpower. Lying is a methodology of life, followed by killing, cheating and stealing. When virtue goes wrong, it touches every area of our lives. The virtuous people need to stand for justice. Now.

In the end, Plato tells us the slave must go back into the cave and join the other slaves for "all eternity" – all the while knowing that, inside the cave, nothing is real. The slave is chained with the other slaves once again and forced to stare at the shadows.

The first thing the enlightened slave tells the others is that all these shadows are not real. The enlightened slave tells them that the shadows are created by other humans and are meant to make humans believe their illusions and become slaves to them. The enlightened slave tells the captive slaves that they had been lied to since birth as they have had illusions force fed to them their entire lives. Human-created illusions are not real. But Plato's slaves never had the benefit of seeing that; instead, they were fed lies.

Plato explains that when the enlightened slave tells the chained slaves about the reality outside of the cave, the unenlightened slaves try to kill the enlightened one. Plato states that the unenlightened slaves hate the enlightened one so much that they will "do homicide" to shut up the enlightened slave. If the mob is ignorant, and you are enlightened, you will become the target of the ignorant mob. They believe they know the truth for them and everyone else. If you disagree, they will kill you.

Many humans cannot tell the difference between lies and truth because of media propaganda. These individuals believe the shadows and illusions cast by the others are real. The media makes this worse with its subjectivity over objectivity in an effort to brainwash you to their ways of thinking.

Rational individuals must stay independent of the others for this very reason.

The unwashed masses, the irrational, the rabble — there are no cures for their needs and desires. They reside in a constant state of wanting instead of doing and overcoming. They are unaware of self-projection and vision quest potential for their own lives. Instead of setting up endpoints for their personal goals and working for them, these irrational ones wish to be successful now! And they do not care how they get it or who they harm in the process. This is the irrational ones' desire. They only perceive things within their heads, not in the real world. This denotes their ignorance and unawareness as they do not see ramifications of living such lives.

I often wonder who their parents were. What did they teach them? How? What happened? Are they unaware of critical thinking in the real world?

Do they understand the difference between idealism and reality? Idealism is what you wish would happen; it is that for which you strive. Realism is the truth of situations. The goal becomes to fuse reality with idealism and make the world a better place — to live a virtuous life with happiness in the real world.

But, instead, the days and lives of the irrational ones are shortened by erratic controversy born of their mindset and lack of personal reflection upon their individual spirits. Instead of reading books, they get their intelligence by "talking" to others. Writing is difficult, but any fool can talk.

Their wisdom comes from their diffusion of truth by their one-sided diatribe. They are sophists and charlatans. They do not read books, nor do they read Great Books, and when they do, they stay selective to what they are told to read and think. They feed on what the group tells them. They do not think for themselves; they follow the unenlightened group.

If humans are not nurtured to rise above the group and become individuals first, they will be wanting for the rest of their lives. Many individuals will die in this position. They seem unaware of their dilemma. Enlightenment is real. Wisdom is real. And so is God.

What is Rational...

Over 48 percent of the world does not have indoor plumbing, but they all want and need cell phones, electric cars, and computers.

Ferd, Doc Bonn and Pauley laughed hysterically! Things are obviously not always as they appear from the outhouse.

I told Ferd, Doc Bonn and Pauley that the puppeteers and their irrational helpers in marketing, sales and advertising seek to harm the rational beings by taking our money and making us slaves in Plato's cave. I also explained that killing animals intentionally and collaterally was part of their plan.

The irrational ones do not really care about people or animals; they only give lies and lip service to the people as they strengthen their business plans. In the end, we all suffer.

Ferd, Doc Bonn and Pauley were dismayed as they began to understand. They could not believe humanity rested in the immoral and evil peoples' hands. I reminded them that over 90+ percent of humans are ethical and moral, but that the corrupt minority harms us all, and that is why animals and humans are in danger of dying. Corruption – in government and media – is what is extincting animals and humans.

So I asked Ferd, Bonn, and Pauley, "Why should the media care about animals if they do not care about humans?"

Ferd shouted, "They Don't! If they did, they would spend their time helping animals and humans, not trying to control and destroy them."

What the media is doing today would have been illegal under Federal Mass Media Law (FCC) only 20 years ago. We are here to help each other, not harm each other over different beliefs and cultural systems. We are supposed to accept each other for our differences and benefit in the process. But now, responsibility, objectivity, and reality are gone from the media. Irresponsibility, subjectivity, and illusions have replaced "rationality" and objectivity in the media.

"Oh My!!!" Doc Bonn said. "That's going to leave a mark on humanism. The media has been forever shamed by ignorance and over bloated self-worth!"

“Correct Doc Bonn,” I said sadly.

The narcissistic psychosis within the media is so deep that they actually believe they are engaged in critical thinking. They believe their own lies are helping people. The media reporters do not seem to notice that we all see them reporting in a subjective manner and that their credibility has already been destroyed. Anyone who knows reality knows the media is not made up of individual thinkers. It is group think and one-sided. Intelligent people know the media's herding mentality is ignorant.

When all people are thinking the same thing, at least one of us is supposed to think the other way in order to protect us all. Otherwise, a bad decision could cause us to fall. It is a sham. The media thinks the public is ignorant. The public is not ignorant. The media is focused on persuading the public to think the way they do. The public knows it and is resisting, but there is little change. People are too busy for change, it appears, as animals and humans far and near cry and die.

The majority of people who work in the media are not individual and independent critical thinkers. They think in herds and wish to group you accordingly as followers.

They are the puppeteers in the mass media cave. They need you to listen to them. The media does not think individually outside of the group. They know little of their authentic personal "self" as they are in a group-think mindset.

Teamwork is good, but you have to be an individual first. The media seeks to persuade you to think like them because it makes them feel comfortable in their efforts in an uncomfortable world. People in the world seek contentment. They want democracy, not socialism. The world seeks to be free and not to be ruled by a few maniacal humans who make money off the pain, sorrow and death they create.

The media engages the public with propaganda and lies in an attempt to indoctrinate the public. This is a serious impediment for children who are not mature enough to mentally see beyond. But go ahead and give them a cell phone. It's okay. The kids are advanced now – advanced passed knowing Truth, especially if their parents are believers in the media's bizarre diatribe. Right is wrong. Wrong is right.

It is just like Ferd, Doc Bonn and Pauley safely coming through the Death Angel Mushrooms on the edge of the woods. One has to avoid the Death Angels of the Media.

The media says their actions are all in the name of "freedom" – no slaves and no masters. But the media creates slaves daily as they attempt to master the humans who do not think critically.

Understanding Ontologies of the Things-in-Themselves. . .

If we truly want to know a topic, we need to understand the "ontology" of the thing-in-itself. To know a thing-in-itself is to know the complete inner workings of one thing. It is one thing to know what an automobile is, to know how it works and to drive it. But to know the entire ontology of an automobile, you have to know the machine inside and out, how the engine and transmission work, all the parts and pieces. All these things are part of the ontology of a motorized vehicle. You can know what an automobile is and even drive one without knowing its ontology.

To know the ontology of your life, you need to reflectively examine your "self" regularly and periodically to insure you remember who you are. It sounds silly, but people that are not grounded forget who they are all the time. These people never figure out complete ontologies about their "self" or anyone/anything else as it takes away from their activities.

"I love education!" said Pauley. "It is so exciting to learn... Yeah-us!"

"Learning is a lot of fun Pauley," I replied. "That is why I became a professor. I love learning. Why don't you tell us about the ontology of being a polar bear."

"Well... a polar bear is more than just a very big white bear that could kill you," Pauley explained. "Deep down inside we have feelings too. Big polar bear feelings, Yeah-us."

I asked Pauley, "So you are saying that animals are more sensitive than they appear?"

"All animals are sensitive," Pauley explained. "Perceptions of humans cloud the truth of animal life. Animals keep to themselves unless they are hunting or feeding. When we meet someone new, we are always open. But when we meet judgmental individuals who use stereotypes to harm us, the closure begins. Yeah-us..."

Obviously, polar bears are quite discriminating.

"We have to protect ourselves in a brutal world that does not care if we live or die," Pauley said. "In a world like ours we learn to survive or we die. Yeah-us..."

Death on earth is not the end of our life, it is the beginning of the Afterlife. The Afterlife is not just an ideal, it is Real.

Ferd immediately spoke up, "I would like to discuss the 'ontology' of an 'ideal' cantaloupe!"

All the animals laughed! What a change of pace!

"A cantaloupe reminds me of God because when I eat it, it tastes Sublime!" Ferd explained. "Well... You see, a cantaloupe is a perfect fruit. It is sweet but not too sweet. When it is ripe, it is never sour. A cantaloupe is in between sweet and sour with a crisp outside, yet soft texture inside, and it is so juicy! I remember the first time I had a cantaloupe. It was wonderful!"

I remember that hot summer day I first saw Ferd eat an entire cantaloupe in one giant bite. Yes. He eats the rind too! Ferd was full-sized, you know... BIG! About 5800 pounds or 2630.83 kilos worth of BIG. That day, Ferd turned into a giant juicer and chewed and swallowed every bit of the melon, rind, seeds and all, savoring it as it disappeared. "That would have lasted me a few days," I thought. But it was awesome to see Ferd smash that melon with one bite. The enjoyment that appeared on his rhino face was worth it!

"I remember that hot summer day too; I was full-size in the backyard," Ferd continued. "The professor tossed a whole, 'cooled' cantaloupe to me that he had pulled from the cellar, and I opened my mouth and caught it. The rind was so soft and chewy. When I bit down, it was the most flavorful and refreshing thing – ever! Juice and seeds ran down my chin as I savored the delicious fruit. Chomp! Chomp! Yum... And therefore, I now know the 'ontology' of a cantaloupe."

"I believe you do, Ferd," I said laughingly. "But do you know how it grows? That is part of the ontology too."

Ferd replied, "I guess I forgot about that part of the ontology and that is the most important part. How it came to Be."

"Well, we planted seeds and watered them and God took care of the rest with the Rain, Wind, Sun and Moon," I explained.

Ferd, Doc Bonn and Pauley are some of the best students I ever had. Their desire to learn and retain knowledge is immense. You have to want to learn in order to live a good life. A rational being needs to know many "ontologies" in life in order to survive against the ignorance and evil that are cast upon us by some maniacal humans. We have to stay strong and nurture our authentic "self" in order to be protective of our spirit.

The ontology of food is another important ontology. Food brings humans and animals together because we all love to eat. Delicious, fresh food is an essential part of living as it tastes as good as it is for us nutritiously. Food likes are similar for every being, yet different. Ferd's, Doc Bonn's and Pauley's needs, dietary and otherwise, have been quite a challenge to fulfill. Eating is their favorite activity other than breathing. They are always making analogies to food, placing an order, or making a request. At times, I feel like a short-order cook. They love grilled cheese and tomato soup. Having it at 2 a.m. seems like a requirement. If I am not awake, they wake me and tell me they are sorry, but... And so it goes.

Generally, it's green leaf lettuce and field greens for Ferd. I have shared some vinegar and oil dressing with him and he likes that on his greens. Of course, Ferd likes his salad better with saltine crackers.

Doc Bonn lives on eucalyptus. Sometimes, Doc Bonn likes a little warm, frothy milk off the espresso steam maker as his stomach gets a little green. Eucalyptus is hard to get, and it is expensive, but Doc Bonn does not eat much when he is miniaturized.

Pauley has the biggest appetite of all the three animals. We know Pauley is a seafood lover, but we also know he is a very hungry polar bear. As a matter of fact, Pauley might eat a whole 20 pound salmon in just a few minutes when he is BIG, so thankfully, he eats when he is small. His favorite food in the wild is sea lions. Pauley's favorite food now is sardines in mustard sauce, yet he prefers fresh fish over canned fish. Sometimes I go through the drive through and order 100 fish sandwiches with tartar sauce, no bread. Pauley loves the drive thru!

We must remember Ferd, Bonn, and Pauley are wild animals "primal" in their instinct-driven activities within what humans refer to as the food chain. Ferd, Bonn, and Pauley know all about the food chain and its necessity for the planet to function within Nature. It's a brutal reality when some animals are killed by other animals for food.

"Yeah–us!" Pauley exclaimed, "I am part of that chain of food. It ends with me and seafood!"

Unphased by Pauley's carnivorous tendencies, Doc Bonn chewed on eucalyptus and Ferd nodded his head, his horn bobbing up and down in the form of a rhino thumbs up.

Pauley's statement was a fact that had to be accepted. After all, it's Pauley's life. Pauley eats about five or six sea lions a day – 50 to 60 pounders – when he is hungry. Ferd and Doc Bonn were vegetarians in the wild, but all three animals' tastebuds have changed since they met me. The truth is, even with all their differences, these three animals fully came to accept each other that night over the vortex in Sedona, Arizona. Unequivocally, Ferd, Doc Bonn and Pauley are now friends for life.

But things were so different for them in the wild. Back there, when one animal was trying to kill the other for food, there was no discernable communication other than "the hunt" for the pursuer and the "stand and fight" or "run for your life" for the hunted. Yet many animals get along quite well in Nature, especially if they are not natural predators of each other.

Humans could take a lesson here. And with humans at the top of the food chain, one thing is certain: animals are threatened and become extinct continuously because of careless and irrational humans, some evil, and many simply oblivious to the problem.

The Media Should be Objective, Not Subjective...

For all that we attempt to do as good, moral individuals, today's media seeks to ruin it all by skewing reality, right along with the meaning of the individual's soul and life in itself. The media wants you to be a follower and a sheep. The media is supposed to report the news "objectively" for the "public good" so people may stay informed on important news events.

The media is not here to report subjectively or to teach you how or what to think about things. That is up to you! The media is not supposed to manipulate facts to create their own agenda and disseminate it on the public or induce panic – yell fire in a crowded theater – or start a riot. But they do it every day.

Today's media seeks to make right appear wrong and wrong appear right. The media today is the inversion of goodness and benevolence. The media is no longer reporting objectively by laying the stories out for the public to decide. The media only reports subjectively based on their own wants and needs. The media does not care for "the people." The media cares about itself and money and nothing else.

"People should quit watching the media!" Ferd shouted. "People should not engage the media as it is tantamount to brainwashing!"

"I wish they would do just that, Ferd," I said. "Our problem is not that complex. If people strive for virtue, they will live a good life. People need to help each other and the animals if we are to live in happiness. But those people who seek virtue as a means to an end of making money are destroying our world in the process. In the end, humans and animals suffer and become extinct."

Ferd always finds it hard to be calm when it comes time to stand up and protect the animals.

"Those of us who are rational animals must protect the animals from the irrational ones!"

Ferd said. "Humans are endangered as much as the animals! Why don't they care?"

Most humans do care, but we need them to speak out about their own personal beliefs. It is imperative that humans protect all the animals and each other, now, instead of harming one another. In the scheme of life, this is how humans should reside as Stewards of Nature. But the bigger point is that without rational humans the animals will unnecessarily suffer and die. Right now, rationality is all that can save the beings of Earth.

Ferd, Doc Bonn and Pauley know that if the animals were dependent upon the media for real help they would already be dead.

Doc Bonn was beside himself, "The media obviously do not care, or they would not keep harming people. I am disgusted by their behavior!"

"The media only cares for profit, Doc Bonn. The media does not care for humans, animals, or anything else. The media only pretends they care in order to make money off the conflicts they create," I added.

The media seeks power over the people. The media gets its instructions from corrupt and immoral politicians and wealthy business people allows the media to spread ignorance and hate. The media is nothing more than a propaganda machine designed to enslave and kill humans and animals, projecting shadowy images on the walls of the cave.

Those who profit off Evil have sold their souls to the Devil just like Daniel Webster. There is no God or Good for these irrational ones; they know what they do is wrong. Good, God, Devil, Evil. Now think of that. What behaviors are of humans and what are from the Heavens? And we know Heaven has nothing to do with marketing, sales, or advertising.

Harming and killing animals and other humans in the name of profit is wrong! Being free is what life is about for you and me. And Ferd, Doc Bonn and Pauley are no different than we are. At the end of the day, humans and animals have a lot in common. They seek contentment. They want to be free and content to live life as they wish while they authentically Be.

Ferd asked, "What is a philosopher?"

A philosopher is "philo" – a friend, "sophos" – of wisdom. A philosopher is a "friend-of-wisdom."

We use knowledge and wisdom in our daily lives to better function and protect ourselves.

But no one owns wisdom, or knowledge, as these entities are shared by everyone to a greater or lesser degree. In other words, philosophers walk through life thinking critically to their fullest degree.

Aristotle further clarified how we should examine our lives critically with "thinking about thinking." Rationality is what sets us apart from the other animals. Rationality is what makes us Stewards of Nature on Earth. Aristotle never met Ferd, Bonn, and Pauley, but I know he would have loved them because they are the epitome of rational. The rational animals' ability to think, conceptualize, and create new things is what makes utilizing rationality the highest good on Earth.

"So humans that have the ability to be rational are the ones killing the animals?" Doc Bonn asked. "And they do it for money and profit, harming other beings in the process?"

"Correct Doc Bonn," I answered. The room was silent. "I know it does not make sense that rational people would do irrational things, but it happens every day."

I explained to Ferd, Doc Bonn and Pauley that some human animals utilize rationality unvirtuously in order to do harm intentionally to make money. Some human animals are more evil than good, and some are pure evil, and they harm everything they touch, usually making money off the others' pain and suffering in the process. These humans calculate animal and human behavior as they force financial constraints upon those they wish to control. Without rationality and critical thinking, all animals and humans are at a disadvantage against the evil ones.

Before they were rational animals, Ferd, Doc Bonn and Pauley had resided in the natural world with all its wonder and beauty and all its pain and suffering. But they did not contemplate it; they lived it one day at a time – as animals. Up to now, they had survived on instinct with their families and friends. They were tribal and nomadic. This was their lives. They conversed through native communication within their species without rationality.

Now, there was something more between the animals. Ferd, Bonn, and Pauley were present in the moment and observing without being disruptive. As animals know, this is the world's best camouflage. Ferd, Doc Bonn and Pauley have the knowledge of the ages, but they most often remain "silent" as utilizing rationality is different than being an animal operating on instinct.

I reminded Ferd, Doc Bonn and Pauley of Ludwig Wittgenstein's last line of his "Tractatus" or "The Tractatus Logico-Philosophicus."

"Whereof one cannot speak, thereof one must be silent." I said citing Wittgenstein.

The animals realize they can think about something without speaking of it and without doing it. They can think and discuss something without actually being engaged within the action. This allows them to be objective in their thinking.

"Before now, I never had a chance to step outside of my 'self' and think about what I was doing. I was too busy doing it!" Ferd said. "I never thought about thinking while being with all the other beings. Now, all I can do is think!"

Pauley Polar Bear looked up with his ears twitching frantically. He squinted his eyes when I patted him on the head.

"I can't stop thinking about seafood!" Pauley shouted. "What are we having for dinner? Are we having seafood? Yeah-us?"

All the animals laughed!

I told Pauley, "I always have some seafood for you! I have some sardines in mustard sauce."

Pauley's eyes glimmered in the light, "Thank You! Could I have some saltines with that? Yeah-us..."

"Of course you can, Pauley!" I replied.

All three animals love food. They have a fascination with mustard—mustard of all kinds. If there is one thing they all love, it's MUSTARD. They eat it on everything, but they like it on soft pretzels the most! This in itself was interesting to me and humorous too.

As I prepared lunch, I spoke with Ferd, Doc Bonn and Pauley in such a way that if anyone had been listening no one could recognize the language game we played. We were close, we were like family now, and in fact we were family, unequivocally.

Life in the Wild...

"Sitting on tree branches all my life, I try not to judge others' positions in life..." Doc Bonn said, laughingly.

I laughed out loud and so did Ferd and Pauley.

"Thank You!" Doc Bonn replied.

You see, Doc Bonn never got a lot of recognition in the animal world although he helped and saved many animals as a doctor. So when anyone compliments him or thanks him he is overjoyed with being respected. That is all anyone wants – to be content and to be respected.

"Before this, I resided within the trees on the Outback, just outside of Canberra, Australia." Doc Bonn continued, "I loved living under the canopy and doing all the things that make me, me! But I only thought about survival then. I functioned on instinct alone. I did not fully recognize my Being as a koala until I gained rationality."

The animals nodded and I asked, "Pauley, what was your life like before you gained rationality?"

"Well... I was a polar bear, ya know, Yeah-us..." Pauley explained, "I mean, I knew I was a polar bear. I just did not think about it. Instead, I lived life to my fullest. Swim, swim, swim, seek, seek, seek. I need seafood. Walk, walk, walk, seek, seek, seek, swim, swim, swim, see sea lion, chase sea lion, catch sea lion, chomp, chomp, chomp, eat, eat, eat, swim, swim, swim, seek, seek, seek. But I never thought about my 'self' existing before now. I was just another being, existing without rationality."

I continued, "What about you Ferd? What did you do before you had rationality?"

"I would mind my own business, period." Ferd replied laughingly.

"Actually, that is not a bad plan, Ferd," I said. "Avoidance is one way to stay out of conflict. But it does not always work. Sometimes, you have to confront people. Sometimes, people confront you. Then, you have to use cool reasoning when a situation demands it."

Pauley is the best at being cool! He is one cool polar bear!

"Before I was rational, I would mosey around the Serengeti Plain eating weeds and grasses," Ferd explained. "I love hanging out at the watering hole and sleeping by the stream under the shade trees. I do not want trouble, but if I have to act, I'll do so with veracity. I use all 5800 pounds (2630 kilos) of my weight to charge the troublemaker. I am the second largest mammal on Earth other than the elephant. I can reach speeds up to 30 mph (50 kph). I can charge them!!! I must protect myself from predators in this world to avoid mental and physical abuse. For this, I go all out! And I win every time..."

"I am sure you do, Ferd!"

In many cases, animals without rationality get along better than humans with rationality. We should remember that rationality itself is no guarantee of good intentions or virtuous behavior. On the contrary, rationality is used to harm others all the time, although humans being irrational is not always intentional. When harmful intent is present, the actions and outcomes of the evil human are displayed.

How do you detect them? The evil ones are selfishly first, right along with their profits. And we, the others, are second, or less, if not last. If you are a wild animal, you are definitely last. Animals need humans to speak for them now!

One thing is for sure. Like brothers, Ferd, Doc Bonn, and Pauley definitely get along splendidly. When animals do not instinctively kill each other, or do not depend on the other animals as a food source, they seem to get along quite well. And now, the animal in Me cannot imagine life without the other three – Ferd, Doc Bonn and Pauley. We have been sticking together for a long time now.

I did not want people to know they were living with me in the beginning. But things have changed, we have gotten older, and it is time to speak out in order to stop the irrationality and insanity of killing and extincting the animals.

Doc Bonn said, "All I think about are my brothers and sisters on the Outback. Are they okay?"

Pauley said, "I cannot stop thinking about seafood!"

We all laughed!

When You Die, Your Soul Flies...

As I said, the Sun and Moon are energy sources on Earth as are Water and Wind. All four energy sources are in the Standing Reserve of Nature for our use – Sun, Moon, Wind and Water. They are at hand and ready for our use if we can harness them. Many energy sources like windmills produce energy while they are turning, but that energy cannot be stored for later use. In other words, we do not have batteries or any other storage devices necessary to store the windmills' generated energy. So the windmills are only good when they are turning.

Humans have not even begun to figure out how to produce and store energy without destroying the planet. Some humans harm others on purpose for profit. And some humans do harm while they are trying to do good because they did not think critically.

"The best policy for living is to Do No Harm to others!" Ferd said sternly.

"No matter what you do in life, Do Not Harm others in the process!" Ferd shouted. "It's the Hippocratic Oath for Doctors too!"

We should all do as Ferd says and strive to Do No Harm to others as we live our lives. Animals get harmed all the time by humans, intentionally, unintentionally, evil intent and not. And humans get harmed as well by other humans. It happens every day, but it should not.

It is hard to live life without being exposed to irrationality. Seeking virtue as a means of goodness towards others is the only way. When we harm each other, we are only harming ourselves as we are all interdependent upon one another. Humans are here to use rationality through critical thinking to our highest ability as Stewards of Nature. Humans are here to use rationality and critical thinking to help each other and all beings on planet Earth.

Human self-consciousness is driven by "spirit", which we notice when we exercise our free “will” while walking through life. It is the same for animals. Animals have a soul and spirit too. The spirit manifests itself through mind and body. I refer to the three – mind, body and spirit as “soul” – mind, body, and spirit make “soul.” That is what makes us whole.

I asked Ferd, Bonn and Pauley if they realized that without them being kidnapped, and without me helping them, that they all would still be threatened with extinction at the hands of the irrational evil ones?

Tears welled-up in the animals’ eyes.

“Do not be sad,” I said. “You know I love you guys. We are together now, and you are protected!”

I explained that death is not so bad either. Death seems scary to people because it is an unknown.

“Personal self-consciousness survives death, your soul is immortal now!” John Locke stated in 1680 AD.

The day that the soul leaves the body and flies from Earth into the heavens is a sight to behold.

“Have you seen a soul fly?” asked Ferd.

"When my father died, Ferd, I saw his soul leave his body and fly into the heavens."

"Oh My!" said Doc Bonn as his eyes got very big. "This is the proof of God for which I have been looking all my koala life! I wanted to believe, but in the wilderness, everything was so chaotic that I had to live one day at a time. With so many needless koala deaths on Earth, I thought the world began and ended on the Australian Outback."

Pauley shouted, "I knew it was true that God is Real! Yeah–us!!!"

I went on to explain to Ferd, Doc Bonn and Pauley what happened the day my father died on planet Earth. That day, I witnessed his soul leave his body and fly into the Heavens. I know it is hard to believe, but the story is true. I have a witness, a close friend, who was with me at the time. What we verified that day at the Hand of God was that the end of life is just the Beginning of Life for our spirit.

I have known God is real since I was able to think and reflect upon it. I was baptized at the age of 9 by my own volition. The forces of Nature and the "miracles" we witness here on Earth show us the face of God. This concept comes from St. Thomas Aquinas on "Natural

Theology." Aquinas believed we see God's plan when we witness the miracles we see.

It was dark and stormy on the day my Father's soul flew into the Afterlife. It was a torrential, Spring rain. There was lightning and thunder all around the sky. On the top floor, the 16th floor of the hospital, the doctors pronounced my Father dead after suffering an aneurysm.

My close friend and fraternity brother and I were standing alone in the room with my father. I was standing on Dad's right side up by his head and shoulders, and my friend was standing on the same side of the bed as me, but near Dad's feet. On the other side of my father were very large windows.

When the hospital personnel left the room, I said. "Well... He is gone now..."

And at that moment, out of my father's left side, just above his waistline, came a blue-orange plasma column, with about a five-inch diameter. It was hard to tell how large the column was because it was in a state of flux as it twisted and swirled up from my father's side. And I have to admit the surreal nature of this event challenged my mind and my rationality while it was happening. The orange and blue column came up about three feet from Pop's body, and it then flew out the window at a rate of speed that could not be clocked on Earth. It was blindingly fast!

When Dad's soul left his body and hit the glass window, it spread out into a white light circle six or more feet in diameter and then became a silvery, white orb outside. It actually looked like a UFO "tic-tac" when it flew across the sky with what looked like a "vapor trail" tailing behind it. The sky was so dark from the thunderstorm that the soul was illuminated starkly against the sky.

Once outside, Dad's soul flew left to right with swooping motions like he was showing off for me saying, "Look at me! I knew God was real!"

After the light of Dad's soul was way out into the dark sky from this flight, it paused for a moment, and then it went straight up into the sky at a 45 degree angle straight into the heavens, in a flight pattern not from Earth, defying all gravity and speed limitations as we know them.

I was speechless. "WOW!!!!" was all I could think, and I silently thanked God for letting me SEE. But with this event's surreal nature, I never really thought anyone would ever believe me about what I had just seen.

At that point, I looked over at my friend and I said, "Did you just see what I saw?"

He replied, "You mean that orange and blue light that came out of your father and flew out the window at a million miles an hour and straight up into the sky at a 45 degree angle, like a movie, defying all gravity and flight as we know it?"

I said, "That was it! I am so glad you saw it too!"

Yes, it's true. I saw my father's soul leave his body and fly into the heavens when he died on Earth. My father was an exceptional man, who truly believed in God. He was a caring and compassionate man who helped everyone. Dad lived with charity and love towards his fellow humans. I am not surprised at what I witnessed; yet, I was so traumatized by my father's death that it took me four months to remember what I saw that day.

When I finally called my friend who was the witness, all he said was, "I wondered how long it would take you to call me."

I will never forget this event, nor should you. The soul is immortal now. My father's life is a testament to Christ. God is here to help you fight the strife in life. Through reflection, humans should strive for right, have faith and believe in the afterlife.

Stop and think of this daily.

"I would meditate on that regularly," Ferd said. 'It is through self-reflection and holy curiosity that we become aware of our "self' and the Lord."

"Correct! Ferd Rhino."

May you have Peace knowing the Truth about God while Being-in-the-World. My father's soul now resides in Heaven. The trauma of losing my best friend and confidant, my father, made me forget the "miracle" I had witnessed. Trauma will do that to you. Most usually "tragedy" plus "time" will show you the miracles.

"So there is a lot more to the story of life than what the so-called rational humans think they know," Ferd explained. "Humans have rationality, but they misuse and abuse it irrationally, and the other animals, rational and otherwise, suffer. It is bittersweet to lose the ones we love, the heartache from the loss of death has got to be the worst feeling ever, but at least we know our loved ones survive death and reside on the other side with God."

Beyond the Shadows and Illusions. . .

Ferd, Doc Bonn and Pauley meditate every morning and reflect upon their Being. It is through personal introspection and meditation towards "self" we discover our presence as spiritual beings on this planet. Without such personal contemplation we are never living to our full potential. We exist as who we are when we are conceived. Once conceived, every individual has a soul unique to their own personal "self." We should reflect upon that. We are born with a soul unique to ourselves. These forms of reflection lead to personal spiritual awakening here on Earth where we may actually see our "self" away from the world with all its human-created shadows and illusions. This is the goal of the rational human.

The shadows and illusions are just like the shadows and illusions in Plato's "Allegory of the Cave" over 2,000 years ago. These shadows and illusions are cast by the puppeteers to control you. These shadows and illusions are created by irrational and evil humans who skew reality to control humans and take their money. If humans get taken in by the puppeteers and believe in the shadows and illusions, without personal intervention, they are doomed, and yet they struggle on, in strife blindly, without knowledge of their authentic "self", forever seeking and never finding.

They are unaware of the ontologies and interworkings of things-in-themselves of our world. They do many things and speak of them but know nothing. They are influenced and led by the others. They are followers and not leaders. They are sheep to be led to slaughter. And the irrational and evil ones are all too happy to oblige the unaware humans. The wealthy, unscrupulous humans who control the puppeteers want to downsize the animal and human population to get their profits up and make space for a new world they wish to create.

The political ones in the United States call it a "republic" driven by capitalism, but they cannot define it. It should be based in goodness and benevolence, but it isn't. Stepping back from here, we see our "self" removed from our daily life, one time, two times, three times – ad-infinitum – and we are able to see humans primarily exist as caretakers of the animals, nature and each other.

When we screen out the evil and irrational others with their human-created illusions and shadows, we see our authentic presence as human beings on Earth under Nature within the Universe. An individual might hold up soul/spirit in front of "self" with spirit to guide. Other than for fellowship, our spirit has nothing to do with others; it is personal. It has to do with us and the Godhead, and our Being, under Nature as our authentic "self," and the noticing therein which shows us the face of God. We have to contemplate and reflect upon "self" and existence in order to do that.

Noticing Your Authentic "Self"...

Kierkegaard referred to noticing the "self" as a phenomenological process of "double-reflection" of spirit, and it's one way to understand our personal authentic Being as it exists on Earth. George Wilhelm Friedrich Hegel's "Phenomenology of Spirit" is concerned with the same activity. It is the unseen "phenomena" that drives us to exist and get things done on Earth. The "self" is that which motivates us in life. Combined with our spirit, it is what drives us to get things done.

"I have always been motivated by phenomenology..." Doc Bonn said laughingly. "And now with rationality, when I reflect upon my 'self' internally, I see myself perfectly."

"I know you know that about Kierkegaard and Hegel, Doc Bonn," I said.

"Thank You!" Doc Bonn replied.

Doc Bonn is right. In order to regularly condition our "self" and notice our authentic "self" being-in-the-world and to live true to it, we must contemplate and reflect upon our existence with respect to ourselves and others daily. To realize who we are under Nature by examining our lives through thinking-about-thinking is our main purpose on Earth.

For Kierkegaard, the depth of this contemplative thinking belongs to an "abstraction of thought" between mind and spirit within body. The abstraction becomes a vision or idea that is created by our individual reflection of self-consciousness and self-conscientiousness. This awareness occurs within ourselves when we critically think towards our Being as beings on Earth within the universe. The time we spend in meditation towards "self" becomes a reference point and an asset when we are interacting with others. When we think critically towards "self", and meditate on our Being within the universe, we are gaining knowledge of our authentic "self" by noticing our wants, needs, and personal desires. When we see our "self" with respect to the others and the world on a day-to-day basis, our world becomes clearer. Personal "self" becomes more and more defined by us through this process.

On a deeper, meditative level, Kierkegaard tells us we may use our ability of "double reflection" upon our "self" to see our spiritual Being-in-the-World with respect to God through Faith. With Faith itself, and the phenomenology of "double reflection", Kierkegaard states you will see your "self" in the presence of God.

"When I reflect on my 'self' Being-in-the World, I am aware of my authentic presence as a being under Nature," Ferd explained. "This keeps me grounded in the real world."

"Yes it does, Ferd! We use this reflective, critical thinking within our personal 'self' as we walk through life to guide and protect us," I replied.

"As I said, when I lived on the Serengeti Plain, my main rule was mind my own business," Ferd explained. "I avoided conflict by walking away and ignoring the troublemakers. I avoided the rabble this way. But when I was threatened by others who would not go away, I gave them the horn."

"Sounds brutal, Ferd!" I exclaimed.

"Not really, it takes a lot to dissuade some animals," Ferd said. "Others are easy to convince when it comes to leaving me alone. I want to live my life as I want – as a rhino. I do not want interference from others. I know my Being under God. I do not need interference from others."

"I, too, understand autonomy, Ferd," I responded.

A spiritual life with God is what rational beings seek. The problem with some humans is that they believe they must be part of "the circus" of life to be happy. Happiness resides inside you, not outside you. These irrational ones want to "get into the mix" and be part of "the show." You used to have to pay a dollar to get into the freak show tent at the carnival. Now all you have to do is go outside, turn on the TV, or get online.

These followers almost never contemplate the meaning of life. Instead, they follow the instructions of the puppeteers. They never think of death or their own mortality. They do not consider death until it is on them, or those that they love, and then they cry out in agony. If you cry out along the way, death is easier to accept in the end. It's called mourning. Mourning the tragedies of life as we walk through humbles all of us. But, generally here on Earth itself, death is a selfish and overbearing affliction that creates the worst heartache known to rational beings.

Also, those who live the solitary life see beyond the fray of nothingness created by others. This nothingness is tantamount to marketing, sales and advertising. In the end, it is money and materialism that steal their souls and spirits as "self" becomes a slave to an immoral, unmerciful mind addicted to money and power. The puppeteers of the media and politics appear here with the dark aura they carry, inflicting death on humans and animals every day for money.

To be healthy in mind and spirit, you must rise above the confusion and illusions of life created by misguided humans for the meaning of life is spirituality; it is not about other humans. And it is not about who can rob and harm the most people through scheming and grifting either.

"Why are rational humans not very intelligent?" asked Doc Bonn. "They have rationality, but they do not use it or think about it."

"They use rationality the wrong way, Doc Bonn," I said.

"They use rationality to manipulate others for their own gain. Instead of using rationality to protect themselves and help others, they malign the goodness in humanity. This harms all the animals, human and otherwise. While the mass of the population struggles in poverty, the irrational ones make a profit."

Of course, money is something you need to live, but it is not an end-in-itself. It is only a tool. Just like technology is a tool. It is about how you use the tools for good or bad. You should never put your population at risk.

"Humans use rationality to create diseases that kill humans and animals in order to control the population?" Doc Bonn asked.

"Yes, humans kill and steal from other humans to control the population never thinking of who they harm. I know it seems ironic," I said.

These humans do not think about thinking or reflection of thinking. Rationality towards morality is gone from their souls. Their energies are taken by their daily "business" which mainly consists of making a lot of money and not caring for anyone but themselves. It is selfishness as its worst example. This is why animals and human animals are endangered every day.

Protecting All the Animals. . .

Exotic animals like Ferd, Doc Bonn and Pauley should never be killed for any reason. They should live out their lives fully within nature. Ideally, the animals should be undisturbed by humans. No animal should ever be killed for profit. That is poaching, just as poachers kill elephants and rhinos for their tusks and horns.

Humans are here to nurture and cultivate all life on Earth, building within Nature, not on top of Nature. Deep down, we all know that humans are here to protect all life on Earth. Human beings should rationally respect all things within Nature and treat these accordingly. Humans exist to bring order to the planet out of the chaos of Nature. Humans are here primarily to protect and build.

Humans are not here to destroy living things for money or profit. Selfish humans try to control every aspect of Nature, often times, without logic or reason. In this process of exacting negative control, humans cause the deaths of many animals and the deaths of each other. And it is all done in an illusory world of money, materialism and profit which is tantamount to a world without a soul. The world has lost its soul. When humans openly destroy the animals and nature, we are destroying ourselves.

"In Australia, I need three trees for myself in order to live a "happy" koala life of goodness and contentment!" Doc Bonn exclaimed. "But if humans keep cutting down the trees, I will have no place to go. With the way humans destroy the environment, I am lucky to have one tree! Humans are destroying the environment with urban and industrial sprawl! There is nowhere to live anymore. And I'm a doctor! If I do not have a place to live, the other animals cannot come to see me for their appointments and treatments. I have to go to them. It makes it hard on me to not be able to help those who need me. You see, the humans do not care. They care for nothing but for their needs and money."

Unfortunately, Doc Bonn is right. A koala in Australia is no better than a groundhog in America. It does not matter if the koala has a medical degree like Doc Bonn. Any koala can end up as roadkill at the hands of ignorant humans. Koalas are hit by cars and killed or left to die every day. People do not care; they just drive on by...

"I believe unnecessary roadkill is a sign of the times," Doc Bonn said. "It's sad. Wildfires in Australia have killed many koalas as well as many other animals. They were all burned! Some of the fires were set by climate change enthusiasts who wish to end the world now! And all because of human selfishness and ignorance. Humans have forgotten how to discern goodness from evil."

Doctor Bonn Koala holds a moment of silence for all the animals who die in unnecessary roadkill accidents.

"I understand Doc Bonn. It does not make sense. It is horrifying to see the destruction wrought on nature by humans wanting to prove their climate change scenario," I stated.

Nature is cyclical. It is self-righting. If not, we are all doomed anyway. There is nothing we can do about it. What exactly do humans think they can do to stop it or prevent it for that matter? Some humans actually believe we can control the climate on Earth. The sky is not falling little chickens—although some people want it to because they need to make more money off you in the process. Profiteering. For these individuals, "virtue" is a foreign concept as their souls are morally and ethically bankrupt. So they strike out to destroy nature with points that clearly cannot be proven.

Climate change is a contrived theory to make money off the fears of people. Humans are so convinced that climate change is near they set wildfires to make it real. And if nature fails, and the climate becomes hot as a desert, or an ice age happens, rest assured, only the strongest-willed humans with Faith in God will survive. These humans will be the ones to insure the animals are protected.

Ferd, Doc Bonn and Pauley smiled and breathed a contented sigh for they knew in the end that the animals would be protected and not unnecessarily die. It is God's will. That is all that matters for them and me. We seek Goodness and Happiness. It drives us to Be when we truly Believe. All animals have a soul. Aristotle tells us so, but anyone who loves the animals already knows.

If people go around poaching and destroying animals for sport or money, those people have lost their own souls. This is so often the case in life. So many human animals act without reflection in life, and they often end up regretting their actions. Why do humans not see the repercussions of their actions before they act?

Humans must approach life with love and charity, with logic and rationality. Humans must not approach life with foolishness, hatred, ignorance and violence. We will live together in harmony or we will all die together in tragedy.

When people believe they "know" things, they actually are in a state of ignorance and unawareness. Most people with common sense know there is too much knowledge for one human to know everything, yet some people pretend to have all the answers to all the problems. Believing you know things, especially many things, is the worst form of ignorance, not the form of ignorance or unawareness when you can be taught, but the form of ignorance where you are sure you know and will not listen to reason.

"Thinking you know everything can be dangerous," Pauley said. "There are unexpected things that happen to us no matter what we think we know. Growing up in Greenland, I had to keep an open mind and stay on alert and be proactive in order to survive."

"That is true Pauley," I responded.

The humans who think they know many things are often boisterous about their knowledge. They want to manipulate others; they wish to persuade you to their thinking, no matter how obsolete their thinking may be by rational terms. These individuals seek recognition for their efforts. They want power and authority over you and others to increase their profits. They seek to make you their followers so they may extort your money more easily. They want you to be sheep. They want all the money. They value money over life.

Those who are blind to the Capital T truths of life will suffer in the future if they do not change. People should seek to live happy lives for themselves in order to attain to virtue and goodness. Of course, there are always unhappy or difficult things in life, but striving to be virtuous and goodness get us through the difficult times.

Rational Beings Are Aware of "Self"...

We gain knowledge through experience. To be an expert at something takes 10 years of experience or about 30,000 hours. There are no shortcuts. Reading and writing strengthen our ability to gain knowledge, and experience comes through time and effort. You can even learn from the internet, if you have valid sources, but you cannot count on the internet alone for truth as it is full of blatant lies and half-truths.

The ontologies of things, or things-in-themselves, describe the very essence of things as they exist at their authentic core in the real world. Everything in this world has an ontology of its existence — even you. The ontology is what makes things what they are as they actually exist, not just as they are perceived. Peoples' conceptions are often flawed when it comes to perceptions, and without critical thinking and reflection, people would never know anything about the ontologies of the things-in-themselves. This means the possibility could exist that you could live your whole life and not know your authentic Being.

Ferd knows all about authentic Being. "Thank You Professor. It is a privilege and an honor to be here with you today," Ferd said.

Doc Bonn and Pauley chuckled.

Ferd's point is if you haven't studied Rhino 101 you need to get to know Ferd. It is one thing to know what a rhino is, to perceive and see the rhino, and understand rhino ways, but to truly know a rhino – the rhino's wants, needs, and desires – you have to know the ontologies of a rhino. You need to understand "rhino-ness." And Ferd is the perfect rhino to study the ontology of a rhino.

"That's Right!" Ferd immediately said. "Everyone should know the ontology of a rhino. More than that, everyone should know the ontology of their own Being. But everyone should know the ontology of a koala and polar bear too. Actually, humans should strive to understand the ontologies of all beings and things in nature if they are to understand how the world functions."

People must engage in critical thinking in order to live good lives. Humans must participate in "thinking-about-thinking" in order to live above the rabble and confusion that society creates. People must strive for virtue and decency with awareness of authentic "self" so they may help the animals. People function better with logic rather than emotion and whimsy. When emotions take hold, people act and act out; often times it is a cry for help from "self", but they do not recognize it, which creates more emotions, negative moods and angst – anxiety.

People who have "hate" in their lives are particularly susceptible to utilizing emotions over logic and rationality, which usually ends in disaster for the irrational human, but not always. In short, these individuals are temporarily, or even permanently, lost to their "self" and the potential for wisdom therein.

The essence of rational being is to think critically. Rational Animals like Ferd, Doc Bonn and Pauley are that essence.

Ferd, Doc Bonn and Pauley are more rational than most human animals. Humans should seek wisdom of personal "self" and the world in order to grow and examine their lives as they walk through it, making changes and improvements along the way. Humans utilizing rationality to its highest degree is the essence of being human with thinking-about-thinking. Humans should build within Nature, not on top of Nature. Humans are here on Earth to help the other animals and each other. The humans are the "animals' animal." They are here to protect and serve the animals, not harm or kill the animals with ignorance.

Rational beings seek spirituality and happiness. They want to know about spiritual matters with respect to existence on Earth, within Nature, and in the Afterlife with God. Most individuals want to protect and preserve life, although some wealthy individuals want to make a profit at every turn. These individuals make money off the pain of the others. These wealthy, manipulative individuals create turmoil in the world and profit from the suffering they create.

The animals cringed. "That sounds like a circus or a zoo!" Ferd, Bonn, and Pauley shouted in unison. "We are not going to any circus or any zoo!"

I told them, "None of you have to go!" Three sighs of relief were heard.

"The media uses irrationality to harm the people and the animals, directly and indirectly. The media lacks rationality, and has become su–per–flu–ous?" Ferd said.

"That is correct, Ferd, I said. "'Superfluous' means something is useless or obsolete – just like the media."

The media obscures the Light of our personal and spiritual Being. This is the core of our Being. It is spiritual Light of Life that drives us. The media wants to put your spiritual Light out and take your money while they give you propaganda based in nothingness – rhetoric that sounds good that is meaningless diatribe.

"So the media does not believe in virtue; instead, they instill turmoil over order, and, in turn, they destroy all Nature by harming and destroying the human and animal beings?" Doc Bonn asked.

"Sadly, that is correct. The media harms human beings and destroys them for profit. The media ignores Nature and the Godhead itself. Today's media is akin to agnostics who believe in nothing," I said. "It is made worse by the actions of the irrational and evil ones as they are grounded in ignorance and unawareness themselves. These individuals seek 'flash-in-the-pan' mentality when it comes to news. They believe that nothing draws a crowd like a train wreck; if it bleeds, it leads. The media incites riots and unrest in the people. The media is engaged in "nihilism" with unwavering negativity towards the human condition."

Interestingly, the media appears oblivious to their own shameful manipulations through useless rhetoric and propaganda they purvey. Or they simply do not care about humans or animals. The media is frocked with malarkey, tomfoolery, and shenanigans. The media are purveyors of doom, sadness and death. The media obviously does not care about people, for if it did, there would be good news at least half the time. In the end, the media will meet their fate with the others whom they have taught to hate.

After hearing all this, Ferd, Doc Bonn and Pauley realized they had to act now in order to stop the killing. And then, on top of everything else, the worst news came...Ferd, Doc Bonn and Pauley found out the Polar Bear is on the

Extinction List too! The report said the polar bear will be extinct in 10 years.

Then, the newscaster said, “From Australia, the Koala is now on the Extinction List.”

Ferd, Doc Bonn and Pauley know they must do everything they can to help save the animals. That is why I wrote this book. I hope that is why you read it.

The Golden Rule is still True.

“Do unto others as you would have them do unto you...”

God Needs Humans to Protect the Animals...

God created the Earth. Humans, animals and plants have evolved through time. God cannot recreate humans and animals at will. The outcomes on Earth, aside from miracles, are determined by Nature. Humans and animals function under this model as do all living things. Other than the chaos of Nature, which controls our world, humans hold their own destiny. Humans also hold the destiny of the other animals and all living things. We find ourselves in this position by birthright. We are born onto Earth as Who we are and at one with Nature. We are here to protect Nature and each other through goodness, love and charity.

God cannot save humanity, but humans can. God needs our help. We have to act now. If we do not heed the call to protect life on this planet, we will destroy ourselves right along with everything else. God needs us to stop killing each other and all the other animals. If not, we all will become extinct. Animals becoming extinct is a warning sign for all of us. God does not have the recipe to recreate us. If we do not preserve the planet, and protect the animals and each other, we are all doomed. Humans need to take responsibility for themselves and life on this planet. Humans must act and do so positively to preserve life for all beings.

Because humans have rationality, we are here to preserve nature and protect the animals. Human animals are the animals' animal. We are not only responsible for our survival as humans, we are responsible for being caretakers of all things on Earth.

Epilogue

Ferd, Bonn and Pauley want you to remember that God is Real. Be a philosopher in life and engage in critical thinking. Have holy curiosity. Regularly reflect upon your "self" Being in life with thinking-about-thinking. Stay positive. Keep reading and writing. Do No Harm – Live a Virtuous and Happy Life with Goodness and Benevolence towards others.

"Take care until you see us the next time," Ferd says. "We'll be looking forward to seeing you! Peace Everyone..."

“The End” Is just the Beginning…

Suggestions for Further Readings

Aristotle. (384–322 BCE). *Nicomachean Ethics.* Translated from Greek by F.H. Peters. London: Kegan Paul, Trench, Trubner & Co., 1906.

Hegel, Georg Wilhelm Friedrich. (1770–1831). *The Phenomenology of Spirit.* Translated from German by A.V. Miller. New York: Oxford University Press, 1979.

Heidegger, Martin. (1889–1976). "Building Dwelling Thinking." *Basic Writings.* New York: Harper Collins Publishers Ltd., 1991.

---."The Question Concerning Technology." *The Question Concerning Technology and Other Essays.* Translated from German by William Lovitt. New York: Garland Publishing, Inc., 1977.

Kant, Immanuel. (1724–1804). *The Metaphysics of Morals.* Translated from German by

James W. Ellington. Cambridge, MA: Hackett Publishing, 1993.
Kierkegaard, Soren. (1813–1855). *Concluding Unscientific Postscript.* Translated from Danish by David F. Swenson. Princeton, NJ: Princeton University Press, 1941.
Nietzsche, Friedrich Wilhelm. (1844–1900). "The Madman Passage 125." *The Gay Science.* Translated from German by Walter Kaufmann. New York: Vintage Press, 1974.
---. *Thus Spoke Zarathustra: A Book for All or None.* Cambridge, MA: Cambridge University Press, 2006.
Plato. (428–348 BCE). *The Republic of Plato.* Translated from Greek by Desmond Lee. 2nd Edition. London: Penguin Books, 2007.
St. Augustine. (354–430 AD).
St. Thomas Aquinas. (1225–1274).
Schopenhauer, Arthur. (1788–1860). *The Will as World and Representation Vol I.* Translated from German by E.F.J. Payne. New York: Dover Publications, Inc., 1969.
Wittgenstein, Ludwig. (1889–1951). *Tractatus Logico-Philosophicus.* Translated from German by C.K. Ogden in 1921. [Reprinted]. New York: Harcourt, Brace, 1933.

About the Author

James Perry has been a professor of Philosophy and Humanities for over 35 years. The professor was born and raised in Ohio, where his work in philosophy focuses on logic, ethics, phenomenology, metaphysics and existentialism. The professor holds a Master of Humanities and Philosophy from Wright State University. Professor Perry's philosophy of life is that we must help and speak for the animals as they cannot speak for themselves.

Printed in the USA
CPSIA information can be obtained
at www.ICGtesting.com
LVHW062346160624
783214LV00019B/286

9 798891 124554